WHAT YOU SHOULD KNOW
ABOUT THE PURPLE MARTIN

by
J. L. WADE

Dedicated to
REP. JOHN K. MORRIS
Of Chadwick, Illinois. . .

. . . the one man most instrumental in bringing about public awareness of the purple martin in Illinois through his introduction of House Bill 1058 in the Illinois General Assembly in 1965. In the face of inevitable controversy and without any prospect of personal gain, he went to bat for the birds with a philosophy summarized in these words of his:

"It is our wish to give full, and long overdue, credit to creatures that nature has contrived to exert her balance on other creatures of unimaginable fecundity and which possess a will to survive that surpasses and laughs at all mankind's skills in chemical formulation."

CONTENTS

Dr. T. E. Musselman of Quincy,
Illinois, who has been one of the nation's
best-known naturalists for many years,
is shown banding a young martin.

How The Purple Martin Became ...
AMERICA'S MOST WANTED BIRD

Many of my friends and acquaintances have asked, "Who and what is responsible for this tremendous interest in purple martins that is sweeping the country?"

It emanates from the sincere, orderly mind and fertile imagination of J. L. Wade.

Later in this book you will read the story of how Griggsville, Illinois, J. L.'s home town, became involved with purple martins and how J. L. found himself in the business of building martin houses. Let me relate some of the activities undertaken by this ardent conservationist and outdoor-lover to inform the nation about purple martins and to earn for him a plaque presented by a national ornithological group in appreciation of his conservation work.

J. L.'s factory in Griggsville is the only manufacturing firm in that small west-central Illinois town. It made, and still does make, television and FM antennas known country-wide for their excellence of design and workmanship. When in 1962 he was asked by the Griggsville Jaycees to construct some aluminum purple martin houses, his metal-working facilities were ideally suited to the job. Twenty-eight aluminum martin houses were produced by J. L.'s factory, Trio Manufacturing Company. The Jaycees installed them along the main streets of Griggsville, purple martins moved in, and the people of that village found their mosquito problem solved.

When J. L. saw the results of this natural insect-abatement project, he immediately envisioned a whole nation freed from the dangers of widespread use of chemical pesticides. Listening to the bubbling chatter of the martins and watching their graceful flight, he thought that everyone in America should know about these friendly, useful birds and how to attract them. He also saw an opportunity not only to do a job for conservation and welfare but also to help his own community's economy by building a market for martin houses, employing his fellow townsmen in the factory, and slowing their exodus to the big cities.

He began to tell America about the purple martin.

If you happened to be in Houston, Beaumont, or Texarkana, Texas, along about February 7, 1966, or in St. Louis March 13, or Chicago March 20, you could hardly have avoided learning about purple martins. Unless, that is, you neither slept nor ate in those cities!

Motels, fine restaurants, stores—all proclaimed their welcome to the purple martin! Cocktail lounges served "purple martinis" on cocktail napkins emblazoned "It's Purple Martin Time!" Newspapers ran stories about the martins. Radio and television stations invited J. L. and others of his organization to acquaint their audiences with the merits and value of martins. Numerous interviews with martin enthusiasts were aired on television and radio. Magazines printed feature stories about purple martins, and articles about the birds and Griggsville began to appear in publications not only in America but as far away as Europe.

Many garden clubs and civic groups throughout the country became fascinated with the idea of beautifying their neighborhoods while ridding them of flying insect pests at the same time. They were quick to join forces with J. L. and his group, and they eagerly participated in presenting city-wide information programs on the benefits offered by the purple martin. Hundreds of housewives arose early in the mornings last spring, drove miles to centers of city activity, and distributed "Purple Martin

6

Time" lapel buttons to employees of radio and television stations, newspapers, department stores, and city government offices.

Thus it was that America learned about the purple martin and a better, safer, and far more pleasant way to combat flying insects than spreading a fog of poison unable to differentiate between insect and human life. We should all feel deeply indebted to J. L. Wade and his co-workers, who have helped tell the nation about purple martins and their contribution to mankind.

At his own expense and without mentioning his company's products, J. L. Wade has produced a color movie on the life history of a purple martin family. It has already appeared on television in many cities and is available at no cost to any interested television station or civic club.

Purple martins already have the heartfelt thanks of all who know them and understand their place in nature's plan. I should like to thank Mr. J. L. Wade for his efforts in bringing recognition to the purple martin, helping its numbers increase, and promoting the current interest in all our valuable wild bird species.

As J. L. says, "Man will help himself by first helping the birds."

T. E. Musselman, Sc. D., Biologist

Governor Otto Kerner at right, shown here with me on the grounds of the governor's mansion, officially proclaimed Purple Martin Time in Illinois in 1965, much to the delight of bird lovers and conservationists throughout the state.

AUTHOR'S FOREWORD

There seems to be a mechanism built into man that, after the hullabaloo of a great technological "leap forward" has subsided, tells him to back up just a little and let his physical evolution catch up with the fruits of his brainstorm. Automatic cooking ranges were devised that removed the need for practically all the cook's decisions except what to have for dinner—and patio chefs sprouted throughout the land. In an age of nuclear weapons, we have revived the sport of hunting game with bows and arrows.

We wonder if this same survival instinct—or whatever it might be—is responsible for man's renewed and very enthusiastic interest in purple martins and other insect-eating wild birds. Libraries report considerable increase in requests for books about purple martins. Newspaper items and columns featuring martins appear almost daily across the nation. Magazines and farm journals devote much space to the subject. Radio and television programs interview guests who know and can discuss the purple martin.

In Arkansas, an organization has been incorporated "for the protection and propagation of bluebirds and purple martins." Another organization, the Griggsville (Illinois) Wild Bird Society, was formed to foster interest in this bird species. It now has several thousand members promoting all types of birds throughout the country.

Can it be that from some almost hidden niche in the mind of humanity a warning has been sounded—a thin, weak, but urgent cry for caution in our present unrestrained chemical assault upon the lesser creatures of nature? Is a tiny voice urging man to let nature take care of its own, as it has done so well through eons past?

Whatever the reason, an ever-increasing number of North American residents are adding to their usual summer pleasures the enjoyment of playing host to purple martin colonies. For these people, spring is a season of delightful anticipation, as the time approaches for the martin flocks' arrival. On that happy morning, a liquid, bubbling chatter from high above heralds the return of their very own gang of friendly, feathered wanderers.

These are the people, too, who will enjoy comfortable summer outdoor living, free from the nips and stings of flying pests that the martins have devoured in countless thousands.

Man is thus heeding an instinct to moderate his use of pesticides until he is in complete control of them. He is now helping nature to invoke its law of balance. If the trend continues, and we must hope it will, our urban and suburban neighborhoods and our countryside will be the better for it.

Why a whole book about purple martins? Is there not data enough in existing literature? Yes, one can glean much information from books already available in many libraries—if one has time to seek it out. Strangely, no single book covers the subject in the depth needed by fanciers of these birds. The awesome *Birds of America,* running well over 1,000 large pages, devotes only about six or seven hundred words to the purple martin and its habits. While this is an excellent reference source for serious students of general American bird life, it leaves dyed-in-the-wool purple martin *aficionados* feeling frustrated.

There was a need, we were told, for a compilation of material blending scientific data with accumulated experience and opinion on questions yet unanswered. Martin enthusiasts wanted, between one set of covers, all the information necessary to acquaint the reader with the martin and to instruct him in the proper way of establishing his own martin "summer resort" and attracting the "skeeter-eaters" to his lawn and garden. A wealth of pictures was required so that readers unacquainted with martins could more readily identify them.

This book makes no pretense toward pedantry. For the basic scientific material included, we are grateful to the many naturalists, ornithologists, and others who have devoted years to the patient search for obscure data in this field. The balance of the material is "garden variety," backyard information gathered from our own years of playing summer host to these birds and from the experiences of hundreds of fellow martin hobbyists who have offered to share what they have learned.

You are cordially invited to join the purple martin fan club. We hope that our efforts will increase the pleasure in your days with the martins through a more intimate knowledge of "man's best summer friend."

J. L. W.

West Quincy Street, where the Griggsville experiment with bird houses began, has become one of the most photographed main streets in America.

INTRODUCTION

Nature, with a wonderful wisdom and sense of balance, has populated our earth with a great variety of wild birds. There are seed-eating birds that help control the prolific growth and spread of pest weeds. There are birds that hop on the ground and search through trees and shrubs, destroying countless aphids, grubs, beetles, and other damaging insects. There are the swallows, who catch their flying insect food on the wing. Without their annual arrival, just at the moment the flying insects first take wing and before the majority of them have laid eggs, man and his earth would be quickly inundated by hordes of these pests.

Each bird type is of unimaginable benefit to man, but he has given little thought to their needs. Instead, he has relentlessly destroyed the habitats necessary to sustain the species. Indiscriminate poisoning of weeds and insects has robbed the birds of much of their natural food. The chain saw has cleared away their natural nesting cavities.

Anyone who wants a colorful cardinal to visit his snow-covered lawn must usually go to the store, buy sunflower seed or other food, and put it out in feeders. If he lives in a town or city, he must be very patient; the wild-growing hedges favored by the cardinal for nesting are scarce—and so are the cardinals. If and when a cardinal is attracted by the seed and begins to visit the feeder regularly, it is up to the donor to keep up the food supply. The seed-eaters become dependent upon our gifts of food. Without them, the birds suffer attrition according to nature's law: only that number of a species that can be sustained by the available food supply can survive.

Swallows, including *Progne subis subis* or purple mar-

13

tins, are ordained by nature to eat only flying insects. To live, each bird must consume tremendous numbers of these insects every day. The insatiable appetites of these birds provide our first line of defense against a terrible onslaught of insects. Without the restraint imposed by martins and other insect-eating birds, insect pests would multiply with fantastic rapidity. Their amazing fecundity, plus the ability of many types to develop strains immune to present chemical deterrents, would place an unbearable burden on man's resources of time, energy, and money.

The current great interest in wild birds is a very good thing. All of the valuable birds will profit by man's new awareness of their nesting and feeding needs. Only man can re-establish habitats that will encourage propagation of many diminishing species. When man does supply the basic needs, the birds will multiply and man's reliance on chemical pesticides will diminish.

Man will help himself by first helping the birds.

PART I
IT'S NEVER HAPPENED BEFORE

CHAPTER I
GETTING ACQUAINTED WITH MARTINS

It's never happened before.

Never has a single species of bird risen in less than five years from relative obscurity to become the subject of celebration in some of our greatest cities; to be honored by proclamation by an entire state; to be toasted at leading motor hotels around the nation; to have a drink named after it; to be the subject of a movie, a book, and a regular tabloid newspaper bearing its name; to be responsible for the founding of two successful national wild-bird organizations; to have an entire town dedicated to its propagation; or to be the center of a state-wide controversy—the great 1965 cardinal-martin debate in Illinois.

What bird has ever been the subject of such attention as in these opening paragraphs of a feature article by Dick Streckfuss in the Bloomington, Illinois, *Pantagraph* in 1965:

"What goes spick-spack-spitter-spee-spack, and is controversial? The purple martin.

"What bird is presently before the Illinois General Assembly as candidate to become the state's official bird? Again, the purple martin.

"What bird, when he returned from his usual winter grounds in Brazil's steaming jungles, found that a whole new aluminumized world had opened up for him in Illinois and, in fact, the entire country? Once again, the purple martin."

The purple martin, on its broad knife-like wings, has soared to unprecedented heights in national popularity and, in so doing, has created one of the most interesting

17

stories of our time—interesting because of the nature of the bird, the nature of the little town that pushed it into national prominence, and the important national issues underlying the story.

What sort of bird is the purple martin? People in Griggsville, Illinois, "The Purple Martin Capital of the Nation," can tell you more about this bird than could anyone at any other time in history. They have devoted unprecedented attention, care, and study to this bird, which first aroused their interest because it feeds exclusively on flying insects, including mosquitoes.

Griggsville citizens have adapted modern techniques, both in propagation of the bird and promotion of the bird—two distinct endeavors—and therein lies the uniqueness of this story. The martin is the first wild species to be cultivated with the same intensity modern farmers cultivate domestic animals, operating on the assumption that there is good and bad housing for birds and varying degrees of quality in every other aspect of bird care.

They have proved that natural insect control can be more effective than the majority of Americans thought, and have used modern advertising techniques—sometimes highly unorthodox—to tell the martins' story to the public. They are the first conservationists to use modern promotional techniques to the extent which has been employed in making the martin America's most wanted bird.

The purple martin, which has swooped into a pivotal position in the ever-growing pesticide debate in America, is ideally suited for its new job.

As far back as the story of man in America is known—either in legend or recorded history—the martin has been a friend of man. The Indians lured it to their villages with hollow gourds hung near their tepees for nesting cavities. More recent settlers have used crude wooden

18

The development of cool, modern, aluminum houses with bright, clean compartments, and such convenience features as telescoping poles and fold-out doors (above) have led to better care of the birds, and a higher survival rate. The houses have also made it possible to keep better records of the martin population.

houses and gourds to induce martins to nest near their homes. These birds have been treasured for many centuries because of their voracious appetite for flying insects and their ability to drive hawks and crows away from barnyards and homesteads.

There are still reports of martins nesting in their primitive habitats in hollow trees but, with the exception of the western martin on parts of the Pacific coast, these reports are rare.

With the introduction of modern farming techniques

19

that efficiently clear away dead trees and stumps and with the rapid spread of urbanization in America, man has eliminated natural nesting sites for martins by the tens of thousands. Since the late 19th century the house sparrow and the starling, also introduced by man, have been usurping the remaining nesting sites on a massive scale. Consequently, the population of this beneficial bird has been in decline for more than half a century.

But the martin is coming back. The tide apparently has been turned by this little town of 1200 persons, most of whom didn't even know what a martin looked like until five years ago. If purple martins have a debt to "The Purple Martin Capital of the Nation," it is insignificant compared to that which all other wild birds have to the martin for inspiring a nation-wide resurgence of interest in all wild birds.

Purple martins, the largest members of the swallow family, are migratory birds that spend each spring and summer nesting throughout most of the United States and southern Canada. They live exclusively on flying insects, and, being colonial birds who like to inhabit man-made houses, they can be cultivated around the majority of American homes.

It would be difficult to think of any habit practiced by martins that man could find objectionable—unless one is an extremely light sleeper. In that case, the busy chatter of these birds organizing their households for another active day might be an intrusion.

Because of their amazing capacity to consume mosquitoes, flies, and other flying insects, martins make any neighborhood they colonize more pleasant. Martins have proved their effectiveness in natural insect control in a variety of locations—patios, parks, drive-in restaurants, farms, orchards, resorts, city streets, lawns, and gardens. The cases on file supporting the martin as a bug-killer and air-cleaner are voluminous.

The martin seems to have a genuine affection for humans and often will colonize more quickly in locations where there is considerable human activity.

They are skillful, graceful flyers—as birds that live entirely on flying insects must be—and their aerial antics furnish hours of entertainment for martin enthusiasts.

They are clean birds, being one of the species that practice the peculiar trait of carrying waste sacs far from their nests before disposing of them.

The male and female are similar in appearance until the second year, when the male takes on a beautiful, shiny blue-black coloring. His average length is about eight inches and weight about four ounces. The female is perhaps somewhat smaller and has a duller and less uniform color with pale gray breast and abdomen.

As befits a bird that is almost constantly in the air during the daylight hours, the martin's wings are long and strong. When folded, they often reach beyond the end of its short, forked "swallow" tail.

The purple martin, with so much going for it, would seem to be in an ideal position with or without the friendship of man. Nevertheless, the species had been in decline, and the reasons are not difficult to find. The bird has had many obstacles to overcome in addition to the disappearance of its natural nesting sites and competition from sparrows and starlings. It is vulnerable to weather— cold weather can curtail the flying insect supply so suddenly that the bird will starve to death in two or three days, and hot weather causes the deaths of thousands of young birds each year before they can leave their oven-like nests. Mites and other parasites also take a toll of the young birds. Pesticides also have killed thousands of martins, robins, and other desirable birds. Numerous · natural predators stalk the martin; the most common are

21

cats, raccoons, snakes, and owls.

Despite these handicaps, martins have retained the capacity to expand their population appreciably in a short time, if ideal conditions are available.

The people of Griggsville, with the help of ornithologists and naturalists, set out to develop an ideal house that would attract martins, and in the process succeeded not only in building a better martin house, but also in opening up a whole new area of human activity—wild bird care— to the application of modern science.

Aluminum was introduced by Trio Manufacturing Company as a building material for bird houses because it is cooler than either wood or other common metals and because it will not harbor parasites as does the surface of wood and other porous materials. Fold-out doors and telescoping poles were innovations that make regular cleanout of unwelcome sparrow nests and care of martins easier. Railings were added on house porches to help prevent young birds from falling prematurely to the ground. Keyhole entrances were developed to make access easier for mature birds. Intensive study of all factors that influence nesting choices was initiated and led to many recommendations about methods of finding the most attractive house locations.

Study of the birds' migratory, nesting, and feeding habits is gradually being expanded to include other species that also can be more effectively encouraged to flourish and to benefit man more greatly and make our environment more pleasant.

The suggestion that a particular type of bird house could aid the survival of a greater number of young birds seems obvious but turned out to be widely regarded as unique. Apparently, it had not occurred to most people that fundamentals known to American farmers for decades could also be applied to wildlife.

At the center of the
Purple Martin Capital
is the "Empire State
Building of the Bird
World." This aerial photo
was taken in the spring of
1966 as the Jaycees were
removing winter door
plugs from the 504-
compartment structure.
The view is looking
west down Quincy
Street from above the
square.

Charles Butler of Arkansas City, Kansas, vice president of the National Association for the Protection and Propagation of Purple Martins and Bluebirds of America, Inc., has had a large martin colony for many years. In 1965, he replaced his magnificent windmill-style martin house with aluminum houses containing a total of 60 compartments.

"At first I thought it was a big mistake," he said. "When my birds began to arrive, they took a look around for the windmill and then flew right on by. But they came back eventually, and now there are only two empty compartments among the 60."

Butler said he believes Trio's aluminum houses are the greatest thing that has happened to the purple martin. He cites two advantages, one for the bird-lover and one for the birds.

The greatest advantage for him, he said, is the ease with which the houses can be taken down, opened for cleaning, and put back up. "I couldn't clean out sparrow nests every day if it weren't for the telescoping steel posts, the fold-out compartment doors, and the lightness of the houses."

The greatest single advantage for the birds is that the modern house keeps a greater number of their young alive. Mr. Butler said in the summer of 1966, " . . . it has produced the most birds that I have ever had, I believe, per nesting unit. . . . I believe I can truthfully say I have at least 250 birds, making an increase of two young to each nesting place."

The significance of what has been done in Griggsville lies not alone in the increasing number of purple martins in the nation, nor alone in the increasing number of nuisance insects that these birds will consume each year. It lies also in the fact that attracting and caring for purple martins is both an art and a hobby that may be

A helicopter was used to lower the uppermost castles in place when the purple martin tower was erected in 1965. Richard Curry, who was president of the Jaycees when the project began, is shown working near the top of the tower.

pursued by anyone who is willing to devote some time and interest to the birds' advancement.

The Griggsville story can be repeated on any scale in almost any state, community, or backyard in the nation.

Here is that story.

CHAPTER II
HOW IT ALL BEGAN

The story of Griggsville and the purple martin started with a Jaycee project in 1962. Since that time, it has involved local Boy Scouts, school children, the community park board, the Western Illinois Fair Board, businessmen, farmers, orchardists, and a variety of state and municipal officials, conservationists, and civic workers throughout the nation.

Now—in 1966—despite the mushrooming activities of the past five years, the story seems to be only beginning.

In 1962, the Griggsville Jaycees decided to undertake an insect-abatement program but were hesitant to push toward more intensive use of chemical pesticides, about which there was some growing confusion concerning their safety. I suggested that purple martins might be the answer, because they eat nothing but flying insects and had shown a decided inclination to live in man-made apartments right in town.

The Jaycees decided to see if they could encourage a population of birds sufficient to whip the mosquito problem. Griggsville is situated between the Illinois and Mississippi Rivers, and the surrounding countryside has hundreds of ponds and river sloughs.

My own experience with martin houses convinced me that if a city-wide project were to be started and then kept in motion, something quite different from the usual martin house design would be needed. I had seen many cases in which maintenance of heavy, bulky, wooden martin houses had become too much work for their owners. Through neglect, such houses had fallen into disrepair and had been taken over by sparrows and

27

starlings. The Jaycees pointed out that if they were to spearhead a program to attract birds to town, they assuredly did not want them to be more sparrows and starlings!

Furthermore, the Jaycees were few in number and busy with their personal affairs. None could spare the time that would be needed to keep in proper condition the large number of houses required for such an ambitious project if these houses were made of wood.

We consulted ornithologists and naturalists, including Dr. T. E. Musselman, a well-known naturalist of nearby Quincy. What was needed, Dr. Musselman said, was a martin house that would attract martins, discourage sparrows and starlings, could be easily raised and lowered *vertically,* would require practically no upkeep, and, finally, offer living conditions conducive to the health and welfare of the newly-hatched martin fledglings.

From these suggestions, along with those of other naturalists and ornithologists, our company's design engineers fashioned a prototype of a 12-compartment, two-story aluminum house. It incorporated features to meet the requirements outlined by Dr. Musselman plus other innovations that occurred as development proceeded. The sample then was taken to Quincy.

Dr. Musselman was so pleased with the functional design of the new unit he asked that the martin house carry his name. The Trio-Musselman martin house, which was to help revolutionize the wild bird world, was born.

At that point, neither the purple martin nor the new house about which Dr. Musselman, the Jaycees, and I were so enthusiastic had proved itself in Griggsville.

Trio furnished the Jaycees with 28 of the new houses at nominal cost, and the chapter members installed these on telescoping steel posts previously erected at 100-ft. intervals along the city square and the city's main

28

thoroughfare, Quincy Street. At the same time, the Jaycees began a campaign urging other citizens to purchase and install the houses. The deluxe accommodations were ready and waiting when the martins arrived in the spring of 1963.

Results were noticeable the first season and were beyond expectations in several ways. Martin occupancy of the new houses was a remarkable 80 percent. (Several owners of older wooden houses complained that their martins had deserted them to take up residence in the new apartments!) The word that there was ample housing in Griggsville evidently spread among the martins of the area, because the city attracted many more martins than had ever been noticed there before.

When the martins arrived, the effect on the mosquito and other insect populations was immediately apparent. Townspeople, once again able to enjoy their lawns and gardens without annoyance from flying pests, were lavish with their praise for the martins.

When the martins left for the south that autumn, the Jaycees made the rounds, cleaning out the old nests and closing the houses for the winter. They discovered some sparrow nests in the new houses, but not one starling had attempted to build a nest in any of them. (To date, in 1966, there still has never been a starling nest found in any of the aluminum houses.) It is very rare to even find a starling near a Trio-Musselman house.

During various inspection tours by the Jaycees during the nesting season, it was noted that there had been no fatalities among the young martins in any of the aluminum houses. These facts were clear proof that the design and material concepts of the house were sound.

With the success of the insect-abatement program fully recognized by the Griggsville citizenry, the Jaycees expanded their project in the spring of 1964. Additional

29

dozens of houses were installed throughout the town.

Among these were a dozen installed in June on the grounds of the Western Illinois Fair, an annual week-long event held in Griggsville since 1887. It was the fair that provided the martins' first big test and the first striking proof of their effectiveness in controlling insects in a concentrated area.

Although the houses were installed in June, which was considered by many martin enthusiasts to be too late to attract martins, these new houses also obtained nearly 80 percent occupancy before the fair opened on June 30. By fair-time, some birds already had young in the nests.

Insects had been an annual headache for fair manager J. R. Skinner. For 17 years Mr. Skinner had used chemical insecticides on the grounds in an effort to alleviate the problem of the flies, gnats, and mosquitoes that "bugged" fair patrons, stockmen, and concessionaires.

"Every year, we tried the latest thing in insecticides, pesticides, sprays," he said. "We ruined food by spraying. Horsemen complained that their animals became sick grazing in fields that had been sprayed. And the best result we got with insect sprays was a four-day-kill— provided we were lucky and it didn't rain.

"But when we started getting martins," he continued, "we quit having flies and mosquitoes. It came time to do our usual spraying before the fair, and we didn't have to do any. The martins were at work all over the grounds."

But the real test came after the fair. Griggsville people are still telling about what happened, but Clarissa Start tells it best in an article that appeared in the February 20, 1965, St. Louis *Post-Dispatch*. An excerpt from that feature, which helped skyrocket the Griggsville story to national prominence, relates:

"Ordinarily, when the tents come down the flies and

mosquitoes really take over, and people complain that they cannot go to the parks in comfort. The fair committee had ordered $600 worth of pesticides. Something happened to the shipment; it was sidetracked at another town and didn't arrive. But the martins did arrive, not only the Griggsville resident martins, but hundreds of others.

" 'One day I looked out the window and the place was loaded with martins,' said Skinner. 'They were on top of the grandstand, they were lined up along the wires. They were perched on an antenna as if it were a launching pad. It was unbelievable. They must have sent out the call to martins for miles around.'

"The result was that the flies and mosquitoes were cleaned out. When the chemical firm's troubleshooter arrived to explain the delay in shipment, the fair committee said they were sorry but they wouldn't need the sprays.

" 'We told him if he could find a fly or mosquito on the premises, we'd order 10 times as much spray.' said Skinner. 'He couldn't. He was very nice about it and took the order back. I still say if I hadn't seen it with my own eyes, I wouldn't have believed it.' "

Until 1964, the Griggsville experiment was relatively unknown outside the community's immediate area. That changed rapidly in 1964 and 1965.

A cartoon extolling the virtues of the purple martin appeared on the front page of the April 17, 1964, Chicago *Tribune*. Richard Curry, president of the Griggsville Jaycees, wrote a letter to the *Tribune* describing the success of the Griggsville project. Publication of his letter drew national attention to the "Purple Martin Capital of the Nation." The Jaycees were deluged with letters from people throughout the midwest, encouraging them in their project and wanting more information about it.

31

Early in 1965, Clarissa Start featured Griggsville in an extensive article mentioned earlier in this chapter, and since then many newspapers have recognized the growing interest in purple martins and natural insect control, and reported extensively on the Griggsville story. Millions of words have appeared in publications of all sizes in all parts of the nation, and have made Griggsville one of the most famous small towns in America.

Governor Otto Kerner declared an official "Purple Martin Time in Illinois" in 1965 in an effort to encourage more citizens to help increase the martin population.

The blossoming of the purple martin story upon the national scene will be discussed in the following chapters. Developments occurred in such rapid succession that an accurate chronology was difficult to record.

The effects of the purple martin project upon Griggsville would fill a book. More and more houses were being put up there and elsewhere by this time, and Trio was mass producing them in addition to its regular lines of television antennas and lawn and garden products. In 1965, the citizens continued their efforts in behalf of the martins by erecting a 40-ft., 504-compartment martin tower in the center of the city, tallest martin accommodations in the world.

Feeling a growing interest in other birds, they also created in their community park the now-famous Cardinal Garden, the world's largest cardinal feeding station, consisting of more than 1,000 sunflower-shaped cardinal feeders arranged on a hillside in a diamond pattern. In 1966, the city administration and park board also initiated their first "bluebird trail," and made plans for its progressive extension.

The influx of visitors to Griggsville to see the martins has boosted the local economy. In a booklet published in 1965, the Chicago Motor Club describes Griggsville as one of 87 points of interest in Illinois. The booklet, the first of many recognitions of Griggsville by travel organizations since that time, said:

"GRIGGSVILLE (pop. 1,240, alt. 674 ft.) A serious mosquito problem and the town's location along the Brazil-Illinois migration route of the purple martin led Griggsville to put the two together in an unusual program of natural insect control. About 120 martin houses are occupied from the birds' arrival in March until their departure in the autumn. Since each martin devours approximately 2,000 flying insects daily, the mosquitoes have been almost eliminated."

Griggsville, as the citizens learned when they began serious study of the bird, was not the first city to cooperate in attracting purple martins. That honor goes to Greencastle, Pennsylvania, where large, wooden apartment houses have been erected throughout the town since 1840, and where the citizens have taken great pride and enjoyment in their martins, except for a 15-year period immediately following the Civil War when the martins were unexplainably absent.

Nor is Griggsville the first community to systematically encourage the martins specifically for mosquito control. The Toledo Area Sanitary District has been hosting martins in district-maintained boxes since 1953 and has maintained records of their occupancy and effectiveness. The district values its martins so much that its employees perform the extensive annual maintenance required on the large wooden houses.

Griggsville was not the first community to succeed with martins, but it is the first to develop a sense of mission concerning the birds' welfare, and to push martins and all other wild birds into the national consciousness.

The following chapters will explain how the citizens of Griggsville did it.

M. D. Anglin, president of the National Association for the Protection and Propagation of Purple Martins and Bluebirds of America, is a retired Navy officer who acquired a law degree after his retirement and now practices law in Berryville, Arkansas. He and Charles Butler of Arkansas City, Kansas, both have had lifelong interests in martins. After a chance meeting a few years ago they decided to organize the NAPPPMBA, and it has grown rapidly since. Secretary of the association and editor of its newsletter is Gerald Dreyer of Crawfordsville, Indiana, who is public relations director for Wabash College in Crawfordsville. Mr. Anglin is shown above with a Trio-Musselman martin house, shortly after the association endorsed the house as the "standard of excellence" for martin house design.

CHAPTER III
THE MARTIN LEADS THE WAY

Not only the wild birds of America but all of this nation's natural resources have a growing debt to the purple martin. It has awakened countless thousands to the beauty and benefits of the wonders of nature.

Once the citizens of Griggsville had proved to themselves the effectiveness of the purple martin in natural insect control, they set out to promote the bird throughout the nation. Some of their methods were as orthodox as writing letters to newspaper editors. Others were as unorthodox as the classified ad placed by the Griggsville Jaycees in the New Orleans *Times-Picayune* of March 8, 1964. The ad, which surprisingly did get several responses, but none from persons who could deliver by the specified date, said:

"Mosquitoes Urgently Needed. Jaycees of Griggsville, Illinois, need 500,000 live mosquitoes delivered healthy and active by March 26. Must be in flying condition. Highest prices paid. Inquire promptly to Jaycees, Griggsville, Illinois. Phone 164."

Maud O'Bryan, the paper's want ad reporter, remarked in her column of that date, "Are mosquitoes livestock? They are to the Jaycees of Griggsville, Illinois, who sent an ad wanting 500,000 live mosquitoes—and ordered it to run under 'Wanted to Buy—Livestock.'

"A half-million mosquitoes must be delivered healthy and active and in perfect flying condition by March 26. What for? Your guess is as good as ours. The price per mosquito? Ditto. . . . If you find out what they are going to do with a half-million flying mosquitoes, let us know . . ."

It's Purple Martin Time

Why People Love Martins

American Indians used hollowed gourds and early settlers used wooden houses to attract martins. Aluminum is now a favorite material because it is lightweight, easy to clean and requires no painting to keep in attractive condition. Aluminum is cool, its surface will not harbor mites. Thus, it combats heat and parasites, the baby martins' greatest enemies. The above 12-family house weighs just 10 lbs.

MARTINS ARE CLEAN!
Martins are either on the wing or perched on their own house — never alight or soil other objects about your house or patio.

MARTINS ARE PUNCTUAL
They will arrive from the Southland about the same time each year. You'll see the same birds returning year after year.

PURPLE MARTINS ARE YOUR BEST FRIENDS!
The purple martin is the largest and most beautiful of the swallow family. It feeds almost entirely on flying insects and is an excellent means of natural insect control. An adult purple martin will eat its own weight in insects, which is about 2,000 mosquito, each day.

Many martins have vanished for no apparent reason except that suitable nesting places have not been available. In order to keep from losing this beneficial bird we must provide suitable nesting places.

The publication of Silent Spring, written by Rachel Carson, has brought widespread interest in our declining wildlife population and the disastrous consequences this loss incurs. There is a growing opinion that going back to Nature is perhaps the best method of pest control, after all. This opinion has brought increasing interest in the purple martin, an insect-destroying bird that consumes its own weight, equal to about 2,000 mosquitoes, each day.

COOK-OUTS ARE NICER WITH MARTINS
No insects! Martins will free your picnic area or patio of insect pests.

Purple martins are gregarious birds. Multistory houses with numerous compartments are successful in attracting large colonies to your lawn. Aluminum now makes big martin houses practical. This 24 apartment "Castle" weighs just 19 lbs.

BEAUTIFUL IN COLOR
Their deep purple coats gleam in the sun — always a flash of color about your house or garden.

MARTINS WILL MAKE FRIENDS WITH YOU
Your martins will soon know you and will be undisturbed by your regular activities about their home.

THEY ELIMINATE INSECT PESTS
Martins live wholly on insects — they free your lawn and garden of flying insects.

THEY SING BEAUTIFULLY
Martins sing, chuckle and chortle about their house all day long.

MARTINS HAVE PERSONALITY
You'll soon learn to recognize each martin and enjoy their individual traits and antics.
Form 4088

A Purple Martin will Eat
2,000 Mosquitoes Each Day!
LET'S MAKE OUR CITY INSECT FREE
Courtesy of the Griggsville Wild Bird Society

GRACEFUL IN FLIGHT
Martins soar gracefully and beautifully around your martin house — beautiful and interesting to watch.

LITHO IN U.S.A.

The cartoon characters on the Griggsville Wild Bird Society's place mats were originated by Griggsville citizens when they first began telling the purple martin story, and have since been used in a variety of ways.

The columnist got her answer from George Mobus, who had placed the ad for the Jaycees. He explained that the town had put up 28 houses for purple martins the year before and had become known as the "purple martin town."

"One purple martin will eat 2,000 mosquitoes in a day," he said. Griggsville was mosquito-less last summer. It was able to give a street dance in August till midnight— and the purple martins stayed up to watch the people dance.

"This spring," Mobus continued, "purple martins are

STATE OF ILLINOIS

EXECUTIVE | **DEPARTMENT**

Proclamation

WHEREAS, The Purple Martin is the largest and most beautiful bird of the swallow family, and

WHEREAS, The Purple Martin feeds almost entirely on flying insects and is an excellent means of natural insect control as this insect-destroying bird consumes about two thousand mosquitos each day, and

WHEREAS, It is known that the Purple Martin is clean, graceful in flight, sings beautifully, and spring and summer cook-outs are much nicer if the Purple Martin is about to free picnic areas and patios of insect pests, and

WHEREAS, It would seem altogether fitting and proper to encourage widespread interest in this most popular bird, the Purple Martin,

NOW, THEREFORE, I, Otto Kerner, Governor of the State of Illinois, do hereby proclaim the 19th day of March 1965 to be PURPLE MARTIN TIME IN CENTRAL ILLINOIS, and request the proper observance of this occasion by interested persons.

In Witness Whereof, I have hereunto set my hand and caused the Great Seal of the State of Illinois to be affixed.

Done at the Capitol in the City of Springfield, this SEVENTEENTH day of MARCH in the Year of Our Lord one thousand nine hundred and SIXTY-FIVE and of the State of Illinois the one hundred and FORTY-SEVENTH.

GOVERNOR

Paul Powell
SECRETARY OF STATE

sending scouts to find where the eating is good. Several martins have arrived in Griggsville, but there are no mosquitoes this early in the season. Jaycees want to roll out the red carpet for the scouts with some choice, juicy Louisiana mosquitoes, but so far the ad has not produced that half-million required to feed 250 martins for one day."

In just three years, that figure of 2,000 mosquitoes per day became established in purple martin literature and was automatically quoted whenever the bird's name was mentioned anywhere in the nation. This figure was originated by me after extensive study of the bird's feeding habits. The scientific basis for this and other dietary claims concerning the bird will be dealt with more fully in chapter VI. For the moment, suffice it to say that I felt the figure was very conservative.

My studies showed that a martin, whose digestive process and metabolism rate are extremely rapid, must on an average consume its own weight in insects each day. Its average weight is four ounces, and this equals approximately 14,000 mosquitoes. Many common bird species must individually consume several thousands of a particular insect daily in order to survive. In the book, "Gardening Without Poisons," Beatrice Trum Hunter reports: "A house wren feeds 500 spiders and caterpillars to its young during one summer afternoon. A swallow devours 1000 leafhoppers in 12 hours. A pair of flickers consider 5000 ants a mere snack. A Baltimore oriole consumes 17 hairy caterpillars a minute. A brown thrasher can eat over 6000 insects a day."

There is little doubt that a martin could easily consume its weight in mosquitoes each day. Although the digestion of soft-shelled insects is so rapid that it is virtually instantaneous, and consequently the contents of a martin's stomach could not be accurately analyzed to prove this,

I felt it reasonable to assume that martins often consume 10,000-12,000 mosquitoes per day where mosquitoes are plentiful.

Purple martins are not extremely selective eaters, however, and will eat whatever is available, including flies, dragonflies, beetles, moths, locusts, weevils, and miscellaneous other bugs. A martin's diet is seldom confined to any one insect and works to eliminate from the immediate area a large percentage of almost all types of flying insects.

The martin's short, triangular beak opens into a relatively large cavity which the bird uses as a "scoop" as it darts through the air, snatching large insects or gathering in large numbers of small ones much as a whale's cavernous mouth scoops up enormous numbers of tiny sea creatures. A sticky substance coats the inside of the martin's mouth, and tiny insects are irretrievably trapped therein. The martin may then swallow them or compress them into a pellet which it carries to its young in the nest.

Although I felt the estimate of 2,000 mosquitoes per day was conservative, it came as a startling claim to millions of persons who were not used to thinking in terms of the thousands of insects which individual birds eat in a typical day. Our citizens still are not fully aware of the gigantic job of insect control performed by all of our wild bird species nor of the speed with which the earth would be lost to insect hordes if birds were absent from our environment. "Two thousand mosquitoes per day" thus became the keynote phrase of a rapidly mushrooming campaign to focus attention on the martin.

In 1965, the State of Illinois declared an official Purple Martin Time, with Governor Kerner signing a proclamation and erecting a beautiful new martin house on the lawn of the governor's mansion.

In rapid succession, several major midwestern cities joined the campaign. Purple Martin Time proclamations were issued by Mayor Robert G. Day of Peoria, Mayor Morris E. Muhleman of Rock Island, and in Iowa by Mayor Ray T. O'Brien of Davenport, and Mayor Ed Jochumsen of Waterloo.

Although these proclamations generated considerable interest in newspapers in those areas and much concurrent work in behalf of the martins was done in those areas by such organizations as the Jaycees in Peoria and the Izaak Walton League in the Quad Cities (Rock Island, Moline, East Moline, and Davenport), the 1965 observances did not compare in intensity and enthusiasm with the Purple Martin Time celebrations that blossomed in 1966 in some of America's major cities.

By the spring of 1966 a youthful organization, the

The Purple Martin Capital News, established early in 1966 to distribute information collected by the Griggsville Wild Bird Society, now has nationwide circulation and is growing rapidly in readership and in scope of its coverage of other wild birds.

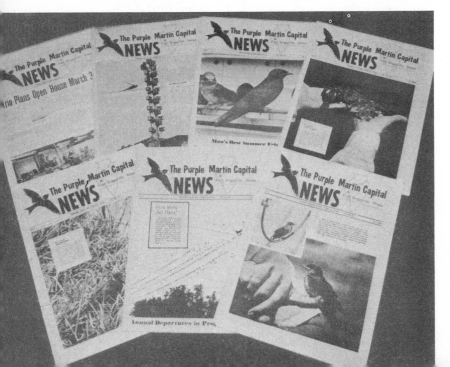

Griggsville Wild Bird Society, was on the scene. This organization, which originally was sponsored by Trio Manufacturing Company, has members throughout the nation. Led by William Murphy of Griggsville, the society is interested in promoting all birds, but its original members joined because of their interest in the martin. They immediately began collecting and distributing information about birds.

Although they were active in wild bird promotion in 1965, their presence on the national scene was not felt until 1966. Before the spring and summer were past, the society had made a unique mark on the midwest and the south, and its influence was being felt throughout the nation.

In 1965, the society prepared material for a 12½-minute color movie, *The Purple Martin Story,* which was released early in 1966 and has been shown to television audiences and civic and educational groups throughout the nation. It is distributed by Modern Talking Pictures, with offices and film libraries in most major American cities. Demand for the film is increasing, particularly in communities with mosquito problems.

The movie was produced entirely by Griggsville citizens. George Mobus wrote the script, Wayne Bradshaw shot more than 5,000 feet of film to collect the 400 feet which eventually were used, "Red" Stead of Stead Sound Service in Griggsville recorded the sound.

Rex Davis, a martin enthusiast and one of the most popular radio and television personalities in St. Louis, narrated the film. The quality of its production and the unique story it tells have elicited many complimentary notices.

The *Purple Martin Capital News,* a unique community newspaper–bird magazine, was originated by the society, in cooperation with Trio and using Trio's facilities, in

41

order to distribute to society members information that was constantly being accumulated. Since its beginning in March, 1966, it has grown with amazing speed in circulation, number of contributors, and scope of coverage.

Tom Coulson, editor of the *News,* left his editorial position with a prominent Illinois weekly newspaper to engineer the creation of the *News.* Mr. Coulson, who held top editorial positions on three newspapers during his career prior to coming to Griggsville, is an experienced journalist, a native of the Griggsville area, University of Illinois graduate, and a long time nature enthusiast.

He became the chief link between the society and Trio, and his office became a clearinghouse for vast amounts of information from society members, universities, experiment stations, newspapers, and a variety of other friends of the bird world. He and William Murphy study each of the letters from society members; some inspire feature stories and others are reprinted in the *News.*

Facilities of the *News* have expanded rapidly. Its office now houses modern typesetting and newspaper-makeup equipment, burgeoning files of information, and a steady program of activity. Even so, it has not been able to keep pace with the expanding information coming into Griggsville and the increasing demand for its distribution.

The *News,* which is dedicated to promoting the cultural and economic development of western Illinois as well as the environmental welfare of the nation, is becoming one of the most vital institutions in this unfolding story.

The demand from society members for information has also played a large part in causing the preparation of this book, in which the first five years of the purple martin story are being catalogued.

The most striking activities of the Griggsville Wild Bird Society members were the 1966 Purple Martin Time promotions they helped organize in several cities, including

The Gulf Coast Horticultural Society presented a purple martin
castle to the City of Houston on the occasion of the first Purple
Martin Time celebration in 1966. Mayor Louie Welch accepted
the castle from Mrs. M. A. Bradburn, conservation chairman
of the society; and Mrs. C. J. Steinbach, president of the society.

Houston, St. Louis, and Chicago. In all three cities, they met with enthusiastic acceptance and participation by city administrations, civic groups, businessmen, and news media. They provoked unprecedented discussion of the subject and pushed interest in wild birds to its highest level in many years.

Although the eventual reaction of virtually everyone was wholehearted approval, the initial reactions of some people and some of the news media representatives were ones of curiosity, skepticism, hilarity, or all of these, depending on the situation. Chicago, the largest inland population center in the nation, is alleged to be a mecca for "con" artists, and brand new ideas are often met with raised eyebrows. The Chicago *Sun-Times* raised its eyebrow on page 3 with the headline, "Cackle Goes Up For Purple Martins," and kicked off the story with "Monday morning was the first full day of spring and the sounds of public relations men could be heard in the land."

The Chicago *Tribune* printed several stories on the opening of Purple Martin Time, with leads like that on a story by Edward Schreiber which read, "J. L. Wade came by the way from Griggsville, Pike County, to Mayor Daley's office yesterday to sing the praises of purple martins—and the purple martini."

The *Sun-Times* editorialized—giving the promotion the benefit of the doubt but apparently still not too certain that it was on the level: "If Purple Martin Week is inspired by promotion, then it's a harmless enough sales pitch, perhaps, and may even have its nonprofit benefits. Somebody's got to provide a home for birds."

Other Chicago newspapers and radio and television stations soon joined the celebration wholeheartedly. Martin Wyant wrote in the *Tribune,* "Move over, Rover! A bird is bucking for status as man's best friend.

" 'It's Purple Martin Time,' the Griggsville Wild Bird

44

Society is proclaiming in Chicago today thru next Saturday.

"The spring festival for 'man's best summer friend' is the third sponsored by the society this year. The first two festivals, in Houston and St. Louis, have already been successful, as the martins touched down in these cities right on schedule in their annual springtime flight from the Amazon valley of Brazil."

It all started in Houston, where the Gulf Coast Horticultural Society sponsored the event, and in Texarkana, Texas, where the Camellia Garden Club whipped up enthusiasm for the birds.

In Houston, Mayor Louie Welch issued a proclamation designating February 6-12 as Purple Martin Time, and in Texarkana, Mayor Neal Courtney proclaimed Purple Martin Time to begin March 1.

Houston, the nation's sixth largest city and one of the world's leading aerospace centers, became completely preoccupied for a whole week, not with big metal birds but with small feathered ones.

The Gulf Coast Horticultural Society, led by conservation chairman Mrs. Marie Bradburn, distributed Purple Martin Time buttons, presented a new martin castle to the city, distributed literature to news media, and took advantage of every opportunity to tell the birds' story.

The Griggsville Wild Bird Society distributed place mats depicting the birds' characteristics in cartoon form. Dinner and cocktail napkins pictured the martin and proclaimed its mosquito-eating ability. "A Purple Martin Can Eat 2,000 Mosquitoes a Day," stirred instant interest throughout that mosquito-plagued area.

The purple martini appeared in a number of Houston lounges. Banners appeared in windows proclaiming Purple Martin Time, and the marquees of theaters and motels followed suit.

45

Mayor A. J. Cervantes proclaimed Purple Martin Time in St. Louis, March 13-20, 1966. Looking on were representatives of the sponsoring groups, George Mobus of the Griggsville Wild Bird Society; Mrs. Paul Dunn of Florissant, director of the east central district, Federated Garden Clubs of Missouri; and Mrs. Robert Bretz, president of the Florissant Garden Club.

The purple martin was more than just a conversation piece in the Houston area. Residents began to erect martin houses in unprecedented numbers and to encourage the increase of the local martin population.

Houston's enthusiasm was duplicated in St. Louis and Chicago. In St. Louis, Purple Martin Time was March 13-20. The ball was carried by the East Central District of the Federated Garden Clubs of Missouri, led by Mrs. Paul T. Dunn, director, and Mrs. Robert Bretz, president of the Florissant Federation of Garden Clubs.

The Federated Garden Clubs of Missouri presented martin castles to the City of St. Louis and to the Forest Park Zoo. The zoo castle, accepted by R. Marlin Perkins, the zoo's director and narrator of the nationally-popular television feature, *Wild Kingdom,* was to figure more than once in the news.

On April 19 it was stolen.

The castle, valued at $75, was stolen—pole, concrete mounting block, and all—along with a terrace light valued at $200, from its location near the Jewel Box in Forest Park.

The stolen castle was replaced by the wild bird society and soon was back in the news. Several martin families moved into the castle and provided, according to the St. Louis *Globe-Democrat,* "the zoo's first volunteer exhibit."

In Chicago, the Garden Club of Illinois did a masterful job in behalf of the birds. Garden club members, led by president Mrs. Chester Evans of LaGrange, distributed Purple Martin Time pins and literature throughout the city and at their World Flower Show exhibit at McCormick Place, attracting approximately 370,000 visitors.

Purple Martin Time in Chicago was held March 20-27, which came during the city's most eventful period of 1966. The little purple martin battled for the spotlight with such formidable competitors as Prince Philip, Vice

47

"America, the Beautiful"

The Illinois Garden Club distributed lapel buttons as
one of its many activities during Purple Martin Time
in Chicagoland. At the World Flower Show in
McCormick Place, Mrs. Chester Evans of LaGrange,
president of the club, pinned the first button on Miss
Vivian Rankin of Morton Grove, education representative
of the Illinois Department of Conservation. Looking on
was Peg Tamillo, daughter of Mr. and Mrs. Eugene
Tamillo of Des Plaines.

Gene Bogdan, manager of the Holiday Inn on Interstate 55 near Joliet, Illinois, reports both purple martins and Purple Martin Time celebrations are popular at his Inn.

President Humphrey, Martin Luther King, and St. Patrick. When it was over, the martin had shoved its broad little shoulders into the number one spot. For weeks afterward, it was a favorite conversation item among the disc jockeys of the city. Chicago's news media and ornithologists are now keeping a closer watch on the martins' activities than ever before.

An unusual aspect of the three major promotions is that, in each locality, the first martin scouts verified their reputation for punctuality by arriving very close to opening day. The swallow is noted for amazing punctuality, having gained fame for its return to San Juan Capistrano on the same date each year, but the purple martin has not been noted for the same regularity.

When the society asked me for the most favorable dates on which to schedule the promotions in these cities, we consulted arrival records for these areas and discovered that, while the arrival dates of main flocks were not consistent from year to year, the arrival of the first scouts was much more consistent, and consequently more predictable. We reasoned that the martins' arrivals each year would be as predictable as that of the famed swallows of Capistrano if the weather conditions were as consistent in other parts of the nation as they are at Capistrano.

We selected the dates for the three promotions, and they turned out to be remarkably accurate. Houston observed Purple Martin Time during the week of February 6-12, and the first scouts appeared there on February 7. Purple Martin Time in St. Louis was held March 13-20, and martins appeared on March 13. In Chicago, Purple Martin Time was held March 20-27, and the first martin scout

Another of the Holiday Inns which host martins is on U.S. 36-54 at Jacksonville, Illinois, operated, fittingly enough, by Richard Martin.

was reported three days prior to the opening on March 17.

Some of the world's most famous restaurants and hotels used Purple Martin Time promotional materials in all three cities. In a letter to the wild bird society, Chris Orphan, vice president of the Sherman House in Chicago, said, ". . . you would be pleased to know all the interest that all these items created." Richard Dumond, Chicago manager of the famous Stouffer's restaurants, wrote, "The Purple Martin promotion was very successful. There was a great deal of interest among our guests and many questions regarding where the martin house could be purchased. Many purple martinis were sold. All in all, we were most pleased to cooperate in this promotion."

Concurrent with the Chicago celebration, the Holiday Inn chain in Illinois observed Purple Martin Time with promotional materials in their restaurants and lounges, and martin houses as door prizes. Some of the inns already had martin houses erected on their grounds and had hosted martins previously. Gene Bogdan, innkeeper of the Joliet Holiday Inn near Interstate 55, observed Purple Martin Time for the second year. Just prior to the 1966 celebration he wrote, "The 'It's Purple Martin Time' crusade conducted by you at our Inn last season was met with such enthusiastic response by all who participated that we are anxiously awaiting the program again this season.

"We have already had numerous inquiries as to when the program will begin. The promotional items supplied by you were quite unique and created lots of fun. The martin houses are very attractive, and we all can hardly wait until we see those beautiful martins in their graceful flight and hear their busy chatter once more.

"I think it would be tremendous if all Inns would participate in your program."

The commercial promotion of the purple martin also

Paul Corey, executive vice president of MoorMan's, displays the Trio Model 32MPD martin house, of which MoorMan's sold 9,500 during an amazing one-month sale in February of 1966.

benefited from the work of some of the nation's leading retail organizations.

Sears was the first to recognize the martin's potential, and in 1964 contracted Trio to build an aluminum martin house incorporating some of the features of the Trio-Musselman house. Sears has been a leader in sales of martin houses since that time.

Two major aluminum manufacturers gave the Griggsville story unusual editorial promotion in their literature. Dow Chemical Company created a beautiful full-color presentation of the Griggsville story. This folder was reprinted virtually intact in *Tempo,* the magazine of Gamble-Skogmo, when that major organization began the sale of Trio houses in 1965.

Aluminum Company of America gave the purple martin story unique coverage in its *Alcoa Aluminum Newsletter,* and its editorial presentation was widely reprinted.

The Cotter Company, a Chicago-based organization that serves 1800 home-owned V&S and True Value hardware stores in 40 states, was the first company to take advantage of the bird's rising status as the true sign of spring. Cotter keyed its entire two-page 1966 spring promotion advertisement in *Look* magazine to the purple martin, printing the background in shades of purple, carrying the martin house as a leading item, and headlining the ad, "EARLY BIRD SPECIALS! Get set for Spring—and the Purple Martins, too!"

In February, 1966, the MoorMan Manufacturing Company of Quincy, Ill., one of the nation's leading manufacturers of livestock and poultry feed concentrates, offered Trio martin houses as a premium item to its customers.

To aid its salesmen in their calls direct to farmers, the MoorMan company strives to offer as premiums only items of proven demand. The idea that a martin house could be such an item was surprising to many persons. The results of the offer were awaited anxiously.

When it was over, 9,500 martin houses had been sold in a single month!

Paul Cory, vice president of marketing of MoorMan's, said, "The promotion of the martin houses, which lasted through the month of February only, was a success. Even though the promotion is over, we are receiving telephone calls from all over the Midwest still wanting to purchase martin houses."

Mr. Cory attributed the acceptance of the martin house among farmers to the fact that, "It reminds them that their fathers and grandfathers all had martins around their homes, not only to provide entertainment, but to chase hawks away from their chickens, crows away from their crops, and free their livestock from being bothered by insects."

The MoorMan success story dramatically illustrated the widespread interest in martins which exists in all segments of our society—farm and city alike.

The Martin Oil Company, a Chicago-based firm with many service stations in the four-state area around Lake Michigan, gave the purple martin story another unusual twist when it gave away martin houses in the spring of 1966 in a highly successful promotion. The company not only gave the winners Trio-Musselman houses, but installed them, too.

The martin house seemed a natural tie-in with the Martin stations, but this was not the reason for its use in this promotion. The company did not use the martin house as a promotional gift until 1966 and did so then because of the intense interest in martins in the Chicago area and because the Trio-Musselman house had proved its quality.

The company wants its name associated only with quality products. Its most widely-known product is its high-test gasoline—Purple Martin Ethyl—so named because company officials feel the bird's characteristics represent high overall quality as well as "maneuverability and quick starting ability."

The most obvious commercial benefit of the growing enthusiasm for purple martins has been to the economy of the little community of Griggsville. It now has a booming tourist industry as well as a booming martin house industry. The latter makes a variety of other bird products as well. The town's businesses and tax-supported institutions have benefited; so has Illinois.

Martin houses played an important part in the increasing tempo of business in 1965 and 1966. In an extensive article in the East St. Louis *Metro-East-Journal* in March, 1966, Leonard Busen described pre-Easter business conditions in his area as "higher than in 1965, but not as much as the reported 45 per cent in some parts of the nation."

He interviewed several leading retailers and asked one, "What is a hot item?"

The retailer replied, "Purple martin houses."

Busen continued, "Publicity a year ago by an Illinoisan who manufactures them, and who backed an abortive effort to gain a spot for the bird as the state symbol did not hurt sales. More recent publicity about the value of the birds as mosquito-removers helped."

The economic benefits from the activities of the birds themselves are being felt in such varied locations as resorts, drive-in restaurants, orchards, farms, and parks. These factors will be dealt with in more detail in Chapter VI.

The ultimate and most vital benefit which can result from the growing martin enthusiasm is that benefit which will accrue to all birds as men regain an awareness of the importance of nature's creatures. The case is summed up expertly in this excerpt from an article that appeared in 1965 in the Decatur *Herald,* entitled, "Martins Have Efficient Allies":

"Behind the enthusiasm for housing purple martins and an effort in the General Assembly to make the martin the official state bird—or at least, the 'honorary state bird'—is one valid concern. The martin is an avid mosquito-eater.

"But the energetic birds for whom their admirers erect handsome martin houses are not the only effective feathered insect exterminators. Moreover, the natural enemies of insect pests include viruses, fungi, worms and microbes, as well as other insects. Our small neighbors live—and die—in a fiercely competitive world.

"In fact, if it were not for the balance of nature provided by these competitive forms of life, says E. F.

CITY OF WATERLOO

State of Iowa

Zip Code 50705

From the Office of the Mayor
EDWARD A. JOCHUMSEN

Councilmen

E. D. Fernau
J. R. Holmes
B. T. Kennedy
Axel U. Larsen
A. E. Norris
Loran A. Wherry

PROCLAMATION

WHEREAS,   The Purple Martin is the largest and most beautiful
bird of the swallow family, and

WHEREAS,   The Purple Martin feeds almost entirely on flying
insects and is an excellent means of natural
insect control as this insect-destroying bird
consumes about two thousand mosquitos each
day, and

WHEREAS,   It is known that the Purple Martin is clean, graceful
in flight, sings beautifully, and spring and summer
cook-outs are much nicer if the Purple Martin is
about to free picnic areas and patios of insect pests,
and

WHEREAS,   It would seem altogether fitting and proper to
encourage widespread interest in this most
popular bird, the Purple Martin,

NOW, THEREFORE, I, Ed Jochumsen, Mayor of the City of
Waterloo, Iowa, do hereby proclaim the week of
April 26th to May 1st, 1965, to be

PURPLE MARTIN TIME IN WATERLOO,

and request the proper observance of this
occasion by interested persons.

Ed Jochumsen
_____

Ed Jochumsen, Mayor of Waterloo.

Knipling, chief of the entomology division of the FDA, 'all the chemical pesticides in the world wouldn't be adequate to keep the insect world from taking over.'

"Therefore, the USDA is shifting a large portion of its research to developing biological control of insects. It is a development which has been going on for several years but was given renewed impetus by Rachel Carson's *Silent Spring.* . . . If given a chance, these natural pest fighters can be of significant aid in pest control."

P. E. Dorsey, writing in the magazine, *Organic Gardening,* said, ". . . I don't feel so stupid when I spend $12 to $14 each year to feed my birds, because I know I'm getting a good return on my investment plus the great pleasure my birds give me."

Griggsville's role in this growing interest in our natural resources is a source of great pride to its citizens, perhaps more so because they have experienced the same sense of discovery within the past few years that thousands of new bird lovers and nature enthusiasts are learning each day.

Griggsville has become so involved in the nation's natural environment and well-being that the society's studies embrace experiences and conditions in communities in almost every section of the nation.

And that interest is reciprocated. Griggsville has so many visitors each year that a new tourist center will open there soon to enable travelers to acquire information about birds while relaxing in comfortable, modern surroundings.

Many persons have recognized the role Griggsville has played, but none has stated it more clearly than Mrs. W. M. Berger, the bird columnist of the Henryetta, Oklahoma, *Daily Free-Lance,* who writes under the pen name of Jenny Wren. She wrote:

"I am so happy that your town is waking up the entire country to the importance of birds in our lives, for we all know that four years without them (Heaven forbid!) would see us all stark raving mad before we starved to death!"

In a recent communication from Bess Abell, White House social secretary, to the research department of the Griggsville Wild Bird Society, in which she expressed appreciation for the society's efforts to arouse national interest through the *Purple Martin Capital News,* she wrote, "All across the nation there is a growing awareness of our natural heritage, and Mrs. Johnson hopes that we will have the wisdom to protect our wildlife and unique areas of natural beauty. Mrs. Johnson welcomes your constructive efforts, and she sends you best wishes."

The people of Griggsville appreciate these remarks and those of all other writers, naturalists, and persons of all occupations and interests who have joined in the effort to bring nature back into the American consciousness.

CHAPTER IV
THE GREAT STATE BIRD DEBATE

The *Saturday Evening Post* of February 12, 1966, took a long and critical look at the condition of American state governments in 1965 in an article entitled "Octopus in the State House." Illinois came in for a major share of criticism, most of it unfavorable. Among other things, the *Post* looked skeptically at the state's interest in birds. An excerpt from the article reads:

"February passed; then March and April and May. The Senate passed hundreds of "little bills" made necessary by the lack of home rule. It decided that well diggers and tree trimmers and funeral directors had to be U. S. citizens. And it showed its concern over birds. At issue, specifically, was a bill to change the official state bird from the cardinal to the purple martin. The purple martins, it seemed, had many backers. Some Springfield bars began serving purple martinis. In the middle of the debate Chicago Sen. Anthony DeTolve— a relative by marriage of crime czar Sam (Mooney) Giancana—jumped up with an alternate suggestion. The official state bird, he cried, should be the stool pigeon."

What provoked the humor, wrath, indignation, and enthusiasm of the great state bird debate of 1965? Why would the legislature of one of the greatest states in the world spend valuable time—time it apparently could ill afford—debating the relative merits of two little song birds?

Perhaps there was good reason.

Here's a look at that controversy.

House Bill 1058, which proposed to change the official state bird designation from the cardinal to the purple martin, was introduced by Rep. John K. Morris of Chadwick, in north central Illinois. The bill aroused no interest initially and was given an almost unanimous "do-pass" recommendation on April 14, 1965, by the Committee on Waterways, Conservation, Fish and Game. The bill had had two readings and was awaiting a final vote in the House before an appreciable segment of the state even became aware that the official status of the cardinal was in very imminent danger. A furious public debate then developed almost overnight.

In his supporting remarks, Rep. Morris listed the martin's beneficial characteristics and dwelt at length on its capacity for insect consumption and its value as an aid in insect control. He added, "It is not the intent of the bill we introduce here to cast any doubt upon the practicability of chemical pesticides to help control damaging insect pests. It is, rather, our wish to give full, and long overdue, credit to creatures that nature has contrived to exert her balance on other creatures of unimaginable fecundity and which possess a will to survive that surpasses and laughs at all mankind's skills in chemical formulation."

Both cardinal and martin backers immediately looked toward Griggsville, both because of my previous statements concerning the purple martin and because they suspected the citizens of Griggsville of being behind the bill's introduction.

I took the floor and outlined the many benefits of the purple martin and the advantages which could accrue to the state if it were to select this bird as its symbol. I cited its voracious appetite for flying insects, its beauty and cleanliness, its friendliness to man, the importance of the blossoming birdhouse industry to the state of Illinois, and the fact that Illinois could gain a measure of uniqueness inasmuch as the martin is the official bird of no other state. Without attempting to downgrade the cardinal, I pointed out that it is the state bird of seven states and, while it is beautiful and its seed-eating diet is beneficial to man, it is of no particular importance to the state's economy. It even causes the importation of a substantial amount of sunflower seed from Kansas in the winter.

The cardinal backers were indignant. They pointed out that the cardinal abides with the citizens of the state year round, while the martin leaves in the winter. They pointed out that the cardinal builds its own nests and does not depend on anyone to supply its housing, that its song is one of the most delightful of all birds, and that it is one of the most brilliantly beautiful birds in the world.

The most heated point made by the opponents, however, was that the present state bird had been selected by the school children of the state in 1929, and they felt it was not the place of the legislature to override the desires of the children.

In 1929, the Macomb branch of the National Federation of Business and Professional Women's Clubs requested that a state bird be selected and that a ballot be distributed to the school children of the state in order that they might vote. This was done.

The names of five species were printed on the ballot. A total of 128,664 votes was cast and the breakdown included:

Cardinal 39,226
Bluebird 30,306
Meadowlark 16,237
Quail 15,843
Oriole 15,449

Sixty-eight other species were written in.

As result of this school ballot, House Bill No. 5 was

introduced in the 56th General Assembly by James Foster and passed on June 4, 1929, declaring the cardinal the official state bird. It was not until 1965 that Illinoisans gave much additional thought to their state bird.

In the June 4, 1965, *Daily Illini,* published by the University of Illinois in Champaign-Urbana, Eric Wolff wrote:

"A curious bit of Americana can be seen in the custom of having a particular bird and flower designated by state legislatures as 'official.'

"The selection of the species to be so honored is usually not a very difficult process. Economic consideration seems to outweigh other factors.

"For example, the ring-necked pheasant was chosen to be the state bird of South Dakota. Nearly 70,000 non-resident hunters visit the state annually in search of the game bird. They spend over $6 million while they are there.

"Michigan, publicizing its winesap apples, chose the apple blossom as its state flower. Kansas, which grows and ships hundreds of carloads of sunflower seed to other states each year adopted the sunflower as its own. The Rhode Island Red is the state bird of its namesake.

"Illinois is an exception to this rule. The brilliant red cardinal was selected as state bird by school children in 1929. The cardinal was one of five species listed on the ballot. Until very recently, not much objection was heard about the students' choice."

Statewide debate was long and although sometimes heated, most of it was in a very reasonable, thoughtful, and sometimes humorous vein. Typical of those who supported the proposed change was John Warren, author of the column "Prairie Trails," in the Moline *Daily Dispatch:*

"The cardinal is one of the most beloved of all birds—

especially to this writer. . . . But I am not prejudiced against changing designation of the Illinois state bird from the cardinal to the purple martin. I am sure such action would not harm the saucy redbird at all, nor make him downcast one whit.

"The cardinal won his place as Illinois' state bird in 1929, in competition against only four other birds. . . . Significantly, the purple martin wasn't on the ballot. Also significantly, a total of 68 other species received write-in votes.

"One point on which Illinois has achieved its customary mediocrity should come to light at this time—the cardinal is not only our official state bird, but it is also the state bird of six other states, Indiana, Kentucky, North Carolina, Ohio, Virginia and West Virginia.

"The purple martin, beautiful and extremely beneficial, is not the official bird of any state.

"Illinois could not go far wrong in changing."

Many who opposed the change did so primarily because of the proposal's commercial aspects. They professed to be disturbed because the change would benefit some part of the economy and implied that this disqualified any of the martin's other merits from consideration.

Comments such as, "It is interesting to note that the Trio Manufacturing Company, of which Wade is president, builds bird houses," were common among reporters discussing my remarks on the floor of the House.

Backers of the proposal were not ashamed of the economic benefits which could accrue to the state and to Griggsville, and some writers saw no reason why they should be. The editor of the Pike County *Democrat-Times,* published in the nearby city of Pittsfield, wrote:

"It may be of interest to remember that virtually every member of the group which framed the United States Constitution benefited financially from the new setup under the Constitution. . . . But does that mean that our founding fathers were merely crass commercialists, or that they were men whose personal interests coincided with the best interests of the country?"

As the debate grew, various organizations marshalled for the fray, but the issue never came to a final vote. Rep. Morris withdrew his proposal, recognizing that the bill was in danger of defeat and that it already had accomplished much of a beneficial nature.

Comment continued for some time afterward. The debate stimulated reams of humorous writing. The Mount Morris *Index* introduced as its own authority a "Dr. Asa Featherwaite," a bird expert who claimed to have developed the parrogeon, a cross between a parrot and pigeon that so improved battlefield communications by delivering messages verbally that it was instrumental in winning World War II.

Mike Royko of the Chicago *Daily News* announced that downstate Illinois was having too great a say in the naming of a state bird and that the city should be heard from. He proposed the city pigeon, which he considered ideal, saying, "This bumbling slob of a bird is, in many ways, typical of our modern, urban life.

"Take, for example, some of his best-known characteristics.

"A person is easily charmed by the cooing, soothing, pleasant sounds made by the city pigeon.

"So you throw him a few peanuts or breadcrumbs.

"Then he takes off on one of his short flights, directly overhead, and the same person who gave him the goodies will curse and shout: 'Look what the foul creature did to me.' "

The *Bremen Township News-Record* of Midlothian wasn't much happier over the controversy. It editorialized:

"Cardinal opponents have compared the old favorite

In 1965, while Illinois legislators were debating a 1929 election by Illinois school children in favor of the cardinal as state bird, school children in other states were also developing a keen interest in the purple martin. At Wilmington Manor Elementary School in Wilmington, Delaware, second grader Barbara Stewart displays her model martin motel to other members of her class and its teacher, Mrs. Anthony Mazzie. Many students in America have become interested in martins as a result of articles about Griggsville and the martins published in the Weekly Reader. (Photo by Bob McDonald, Wilmington, Delaware)

to the state bird of South Dakota, the ring-necked pheasant. Opponents feel the cardinal just doesn't attract the money men who hunt the pheasant and spend $7 million in South Dakota doing so each year.

"O.K., so the cardinal isn't exactly a hunter's challenge, but then we can't fancy many outdoorsmen getting wild about purple martin under glass, either.

"Other state birds are Oklahoma's scissor-tailed fly-catcher and Minnesota's loon.

"We don't want others to go around calling us 'crazy' as one, nor do we particularly care about the originality factor of the scissor-tailed flycatcher—that is, unless someone comes up with the ruffle-butted mosquito eater.

"There we can see progress."

The gifted pens of the news media may never again be silent on the subject of birds. Long after the state bird controversy had taken its official place in history, the martin was still occupying a prominent place in the news and editorial columns. It still inspires a variety of comment, although most of it is more enthusiastic than that of an editorial writer for the Lindsey-Schaub newspapers, a lively group that serves nearly all of southern Illinois from its vantage points in Champaign-Urbana, Decatur, East St. Louis, and Carbondale. He still was not entirely convinced of the value of the bird controversy and unleashed a bit of satire early in 1966:

"What do Illinoisans do while the purple martin is south for the winter?

"They write full page advertisements in New York papers urging industries to leave that unlighted, traffic-jammed, watershort metropolis and come to Illinois.

"They contend for the title of most vociferous opponent to holding a world heavyweight title boxing match within the state's borders.

"They exchange pleasantries with their neighboring state

to the north regarding the location of the cradle from which sprang the GOP.

"Hopefully, a good thaw and a strong March wind will end the Silly Season.

"At any rate those purple martins shouldn't have any trouble finding their way back to Illinois this spring. The state has spent the entire winter trying to put itself on the map."

Nevertheless, many looked back with genuine appreciation for the great good resulting from the debate. While the purple martin still is not any state's official bird, all birds—especially in Illinois—are better off than they were a year earlier.

The controversy of 1965 provoked humor, wrath, indignation, and enthusiasm—and a new interest in birds. After a year, the intense emotions have faded from even the most fervent supporters of the two birds, but the genuine widespread interest in birds which was aroused continues to grow every day. In retrospect, even those who condemned House Bill 1058 most heartily now recognize the benefits that resulted.

Many echo the sentiments of Russell Carter, a naturalist of Schenectady, New York, and an Illinoisan by birth. He recently wrote that while he did "have to admit to a certain reticence to go along with the business then afoot to downgrade the cardinal. . . . I do commend the Trio organization for original and significant contributions to the conservation of a valuable asset in our communities across the nation. The voices of the martins and the cardinals too often have been stilled rather than heard in the name of human progress."

A new tourist center and the Griggsville Wild Bird Society's new research center both are located in the Purple Martin Capital Building, a modern office building on West Quincy Street in Griggsville. This building also houses offices of several businesses.

CHAPTER V
THE PEOPLE KEEP IT MOVING

Many civic clubs have recognized the purple martin program as an ideal way to help their communities while helping their organizational treasuries. Purple martins have been a natural for civic clubs since the first day of the modern purple martin promotion concept.

The Griggsville Jaycees were instrumental in originating and launching the idea, and appropriately enough, were also instrumental in alerting other civic clubs to the purple martin's potential.

In 1964, after the previous year's success had boosted purple martin interest in Griggsville, the Jaycees initiated "Operation Purple Martin Alert." Before it was over, they had more people watching the sky than at any time since the first flying saucer alarm.

The Jaycees acquired from their national headquarters in Tulsa the names of state presidents of other nationally-organized service clubs. Then they wrote to those officials and acquired the addresses of individual club officers in their respective states. They wrote to these clubs, requesting their participation in a unique program.

In letters to newspapers in these participating communities, the Jaycees outlined the success of the Griggsville project, discussed the migratory habits of the birds, and asked the papers to cooperate in seeking arrival dates. Many newspapers carried the following story in the late winter of 1964:

"Attention, all spring wishers, bird lovers and mosquito-bite scratchers! An urgent request has come from the Jaycees of Griggsville, Illinois, for all citizens—wherever they may be—to keep an eye on the sky, the nearest telephone line or, even a martin house that might be in the neighborhood. The moment any person sees a glossy, blue-black bird measuring approximately 8″ in length and sporting a forked "swallow" tail either swooping gracefully through the air or perched on the afore-mentioned phone line or martin house—please telephone this newspaper AT ONCE!

"Immediately upon receiving this report of a purple martin sighting this paper will let its readers know that: Spring is really here! 2. Spring *will not* be silent! 3. Mosquitoes BEWARE—the purple martins are here!

"How do the Griggsville, Illinois, Jaycees fit into this important spring event and what in the world are purple martins, anyway?"

After briefly explaining the success of the Griggsville project, the article continued:

"One of the most frequently asked questions, according to Richard Curry, president of the Griggsville Jaycees, is 'When do the purple martin scouts appear in my area?' It seems that this information is vital because of two reasons: First, the arrival of the purple martin scouts is, according to many naturalists, the most accurate evidence of spring there can be. Purple martins eat only flying insects and cannot exist for more than 48 hours without plentiful supply of this food. Therefore, when the martins show up we know the weather will be mild enough to send clouds of insects into the air.

"Second, the appearance of the martin scouts is the clarion call to purple martin 'hobbyists' to get their houses installed and hang out the 'for rent' sign. Their purpose, of course, is to entice the martins to spend the summer in their yards and feast upon the myriad mosquitoes, beetles, flies and other flying pests that could and would,

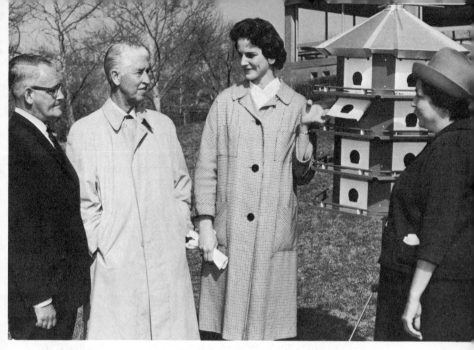

Marlin Perkins, director of Forest Park Zoo in St. Louis and narrator of the television feature, "Wild Kingdom," accepted a martin castle for the zoo, which later produced the zoo's first "volunteer exhibit." Making the presentation were Mr. Mobus, Mrs. Bretz, and Mrs. Dunn.

if allowed, mess up many a cook-out, patio party or other summertime outdoor activity.

"So the Griggsville Jaycees are asking this newspaper to ask our readers to join in Operation Purple Martin Alert! You let us know when the very first martin scout makes his appearance and this paper will gratefully spread the word . . . SPRING IS HERE!"

(Actually, we now know that the appearance of the flocks, not necessarily the first scout, is the true sign of spring.)

Operation Purple Martin Alert was a great success and started the Griggsville citizens on the way to collecting the wealth of information from all parts of the

71

country that now fills their files and furnishes a foundation for the society's research program.

The scheme not only made the average citizen aware of the martin's existence; it also alerted civic clubs to the martin's possibilities as a community service project.

Since that time the organizations and areas which have participated in the program are as diverse as the Massachusetts Audubon Society; the Mercer County Conservation District in Trenton, New Jersey; the Young Men's Business Club of Lake Charles, Louisiana; the South Side Optimists of Fort Wayne, Indiana; and the Jaycees of Saratoga, Wyoming.

The majority of the projects have been successful. Communities have reported larger numbers of martins and fewer insects. Some have reported spectacular successes.

In some cases, success was delayed a year or more by inclement weather, which reduced the number of martins in certain regions. In Philipsburg, Pennsylvania, for example, the Kiwanis, Chamber of Commerce, and municipal government erected houses in 1966 but, because of the weather reported no more than 50 martins in the city. Philipsburg is located only about 100 miles north of the famed Greencastle colony, so the city is still optimistic about next spring. Their optimism will become reality with patience.

One of the first successful civic club projects was initiated by the Lions of Salina, Kansas, who have been installing martin houses and distributing literature for three years. They report that the project's popularity has not diminished.

In Danville, Kentucky, the Little Garden Club may have the first successful project to be initiated as a direct result of the municipality's investigation of chemical insect control. Club members, concerned about a possible

72

The Lombard, Illinois, Jaycees used their 1918 LaFrance firetruck to publicize their martin house campaign, which they conducted in cooperation with their local distributor. Shown on the truck are (left to right) Ted Roepe, Jack Bitter, "Little Jack" Bitter, Bill Templeman, and Bill Riddle. Purple Martin Control Center was set up in a tent, where the movie, "The Purple Martin Story," was shown and martin houses were displayed. Jaycee Steve Wilk is shown in lower right photo inspecting a castle. Jaycees sold more than 200 houses in the campaign, despite a late start in the season.

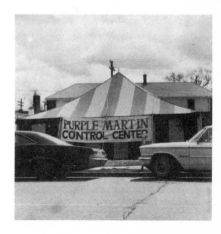

municipally-sponsored pesticide program, suggested that martins should be given a chance instead. Mrs. Donald M. Arnaud, the club's president, said the group itself put up 68 aluminum houses, and other citizens put up half again as many. Martins were attracted the first season, and some of the houses were nearly full, she said.

Some newspapers themselves have actively promoted martin houses as a community service. James M. Savell of the East Prairie *Eagle* in East Prairie, Missouri (population 4,000), promoted 56 aluminum martin houses in his community, personally assembling 54 of them for friends, and recently reported, "Of the 56 houses in East Prairie, 52 had martins, some completely filled and others two, six, eight or more."

The first conservation district to undertake a successful major program is the North Cook County Conservation District headquartered in Barrington, Illinois. The program, under the direction of Frank Wollney, made Barrington and surrounding communities among the most martin-conscious of the nation.

The Toledo, Ohio, project sponsored and maintained by the Toledo Area Sanitary District, is now 12 years old.

In its editorial column of March 3, 1965, the *Chicago's American* recognized the efforts of Neptune, New Jersey:

"Officials of the northwest and south mosquito abatement districts of Cook County might be interested to know Neptune, New Jersey, officials plan to combat mosquitoes this summer by populating the community with insect-eating birds.

"A colony of birdhouses will be built to accommodate purple martins, who enjoy large quantities of mosquitoes in their diet. In addition, the board of health is waging a campaign to eliminate stagnant water ponds where the insects breed.

74

"Using natural checks on pest populations strikes us as far superior to mosquito abatement district practices of indiscriminately spraying insecticides over large residential areas. The poison sprays have been found to be just as deadly to song birds as insects, and debate as to whether they are detrimental to human health is still continuing.

"We think most people would prefer the sight of martins dipping thru the skies and the song of birds to the hiss of the sprayer. Such a program would also save the taxpayer money now spent on expensive chemicals and probably provide better controls. At least, it should be given a try."

This kind of editorial support and receptiveness to new ideas has contributed immeasurably to the growing

One of the most gratifying moments of my life occurred at the 1965 convention of the NAPPPMBA in Indianapolis. I received a plaque from the group in appreciation of our city's work in behalf of purple martins, and I was given the title of "The Purple Martin King." Dr. T. E. Musselman made the presentation, which made the moment an even greater honor.

national interest in natural insect control. None of the community projects begun during the past three years has been abandoned. On the contrary, most have been expanded, even though some were initiated against strong opposition from interests promoting complete and massive chemical insect destruction.

The Grand Rapids Audubon Society has publicly acknowledged the debt which all birds have to the purple martin. In the case of the Grand Rapids organization, the purple martin is benefitting other birds in more ways than one. A few years ago, the Grand Rapids society initiated "Bluebirds Unlimited," a program to provide low-cost bluebird houses throughout the midwest. By the end of 1966, this program will have been responsible for erecting 10,000 new bluebird houses and for a tremendous increase in the number of midwestern bluebirds.

These houses are provided at just a few cents above cost—the profit defraying the cost of distributing information—and the project has been breaking even at best and losing money at times.

The greatest obstacle to the promotion of bluebird houses is the species' practice of nesting exclusively in the countryside, no closer to populated areas than the community's fringe. For this reason, many people are reluctant to devote time and money to their welfare. The martin house has helped overcome this problem in the Grand Rapids project.

Last year, the club undertook the sale of aluminum martin houses, with all profits earmarked to promote its bluebird houses. The program has been a growing success since its beginning.

Raleigh Stotz, director of "Bluebirds Unlimited," commented at the 1966 NAPPPMBA convention in Pekin, Illinois, "It looks like the purple martin will be a city bird that supports its country cousin."

76

CHAPTER VI
THE MARTIN PROVES ITSELF

During the last five years, evidence that natural means of insect control can be both effective and pleasant has continued to accumulate.

Griggsville's experience alone would be impressive, but developments at LaVerne, Iowa, and Walnut Ridge, Arkansas, are equally convincing. These were the first two communities to undertake an insect control program after the success of the Griggsville project.

At LaVerne, a community of 600, the village board purchased and erected 14 martin houses prior to the 1964 nesting season. At the same time, they laid out a program of controlled spraying, weed control and mowing, and proper garbage collection and disposal. The surprising success of the martin campaign in its first season is described in a letter from Mayor James L. Mallory:

"Last spring, our town purchased $200 worth of insect spray, and as of this date we have not used $25 of this spray.

"All totalled, we put up 14 of your 12-compartment houses, and we had occupancy in all but one house, and some houses had as many as eight pair. We feel that next year we will have very near 100 percent. It is already on the agenda of our town council to order 12 more of your houses.

"Our town had mixed emotions this spring about martins, but after this summer and our near mosquito-free evenings and no spraying, our town is quite enthusiastic about the promotion of a martin house for every block."

Walnut Ridge, Arkansas, a community of 3,500, began

an extensive purple martin project the same year. In May of 1965, Jim Bland Jr., editor of the *Times Dispatch* in that city, wrote:

". . . I guess we have 500 boxes in town and a surprising number of martins. Except in areas where there are lots of trees, most houses have martins. My 12-apartment box was one of the first up, and I didn't have any martins until about the middle of last week. I have seven now, nesting and working.

"We have no mosquitoes. When I ask someone about this, they affirm that they have no mosquitoes, and then we start to wonder if the martins had anything to do with it. Suffice it to say that for the first time in many years, mosquitoes are not now a problem here. We have had lots of rain in the past two weeks, and those who do not attribute the lack of pests to the martins are at a loss to explain the cause of the change."

The explanation was available as long ago as 1907, when Neltje Blanchen wrote in the book, *Birds Every Child Should Know:* "Intelligent people, who are only just beginning to realize what birds do for us and how very much more they might be induced to do, are putting up boxes for the martins, not only near their own houses, that the birds may rid the air of mosquitoes, but in their gardens and orchards that incalculable numbers of injurious pests in the winged stage may be destroyed."

Roger Peterson, in Leaflet No. 13 of the Audubon Society, states ". . . they must often travel great distances to satisfy the demands of their young for all sorts of beetles, locusts, flies, mosquitoes, and other flying insects."

National Museum Bulletin 179 states:

"The whole diet of the purple martin can be fully covered by one word—insects! When that is said, all is said, for that is what the bird subsists upon and nothing else."

Colonies of purple martins are becoming increasingly recognized as economic boons to city and farm residents alike.

The bulletin then quotes Prof. F. E. L. Beal's studies of the martin's diet, which lists flies; stink bugs; tree hoppers; negro bugs; May, ground, dung, cotton boll and clover weevil beetles; moths and butterflies; dragonflies; and other bugs. Prof. Beal states, "Martins are said to feed heavily at times on mosquitoes . . . In some instances a great decrease of mosquitoes is said to have followed the establishment of martin colonies, but I have had no opportunity to investigate these reports."

The bulletin then concludes, "Certainly it would be logical to suppose that the area about a thriving martin colony would be freer of mosquitoes than one without these birds."

Martin enthusiasts who can vouch for that conclusion now number in the thousands and are increasing with the establishment of each new martin colony. Countless

Americans credit the martin with eliminating insects around their homes and gardens and making them more pleasant.

A typical comment is that of George Pheasant of Plainfield, Indiana, who said, "With the lake, the fields, and woods close by, we certainly have a fine place for insects and bugs to thrive. But our martins seem to keep the air mighty free of insects, and it is a pleasure to sit on the patio or have a cookout without having to spray insect repellent or wear a net."

One of the first experiences to come to our attention was that of E. R. Alden of New York City who installed a 12-compartment house at his country place near Bear Lake at Stockton, New York, in April, 1963. When his family returned in June that year, they found martins in residence and reported, "They indeed were a joy to watch and listen to, and incidentally, we were singularly free of insects by comparison with a nearby neighbor."

Mrs. E. C. Shaver of Houston, Texas, who has worked diligently to promote martins in that area, played a key role in the city-wide Purple Martin Time in Houston in 1966, and is as good a friend as the martins have in this country, has three houses with 44 compartments, and had approximately 80 martins at her home in 1966.

"Before I put up my martin house," said Mrs. Shaver, "the mosquitoes were so bad at our house we couldn't stay outside very much. When I went to work in my garden, the mosquitoes were so bad I couldn't work but a few minutes at a time. Now we hardly ever see a mosquito around our house. Just think, if you only have eight martins, and they each eat 2,000 mosquitoes a day, that is 16,000 mosquitoes a day gone from your home. Spraying once a week couldn't do much better than that."

One of the largest martin colonies in the Jackson, Mississippi, area inhabits a 34-compartment house at the home of Kenneth W. Drake. It took only three years to fill the house to capacity, and the insect control the martins brought with them is noticeable. The Jackson *Clarion-Ledger* reported:

"Drake says there are side benefits to having bird houses in a yard. First, naturally, is a chance to watch the feathered friends at work and play. But doubly important is the fact that in a yard where 34 martin families are housed, there is a noticeable cleaning up, constantly, of insects. The Drakes just don't have them."

Martins are useful in far more situations than lawns and gardens alone. Businessmen and recreation managers throughout the nation are finding an ever-increasing list of uses for them.

At Bismarck, Missouri, Gloria and Gus Bell have a colony at the Lady Queen motel and drive-in restaurant, which they own and operate. They raise approximately 200 martins in their colony every year.

Bell recently said, "About seven years ago, I put up three martin houses and had very good luck and filled all of them. I have a drive-in restaurant and motel, and no bug problem, anymore, but before I got my martins I have seen the time I could not serve out of my outside serving windows at night."

In Macomb, Illinois, Willard Chapman, who operates Chapman's Mobile Manor, installed 11 martin houses, and in 1966 had at least 50 occupants. Mr. Chapman said he "did not feel it was necessary to use insecticides this year. The patrons also enjoyed the birds and have been very complimentary. . . ."

In Jacksonville, Illinois, Richard Martin of the Holiday Inn said that in addition to helping free the air of insects, his "martins would often stay up beyond the usual bed time in order to watch the folks frolicking around the pool. Purple martins are great 'people watchers'."

Of course, Mr. Martin may have been prejudiced in favor of other martins.

So, too, may be Laura A. Delaney of Hobe Sound, Florida, who said, "These specific birds are more effective than our county mosquito control." She lives in Martin County, Florida.

"Timber" Dahlberg, who operates Timber's Resort at Howard Lake, Minnesota, believes martins are one of the important factors in the success of his resort. According to Dahlberg, "Martins are the key birds here at my resort. I have four houses that comprise some 130 nesting compartments which annually nest in excess of 100 pairs. Besides their esthetic value, may I assure you that we have no insect problem here!"

Martin houses are in use at the Plum Island Wildlife Refuge near Rowley, Massachusetts, and William French, manager of the refuge, is one of the area's greatest boosters of martins as a means of mosquito control. He has encouraged all citizens of his area to erect houses in an effort to build large colonies. More about the purple martins in Massachusetts and the remainder of New England will be discussed in a later chapter dealing with the bird's distribution in that area.

Martin houses are being used in ever-increasing numbers in parks, zoos, recreation areas, and preserves across the country, being used both for insect control and the natural interest and beauty they add to such areas. Among these are Cypress Gardens near Lakeland, Florida; International Friendship Gardens at Michigan City, Indiana; Forest Park Zoo in St. Louis; Lincoln Park Zoo in Chicago; Swiss Pines Refuge near Malvern, Pennsylvania; and the Cornell University campus at Ithaca, New York, all of which have beautiful Trio aluminum houses.

One of the latest and most unusual testimonials to the martin's importance came from the Greater St. Louis

Veterinary Association, which encouraged the care of martins as a favor to other pets, especially dogs. The St. Louis *Globe-Democrat* outlined their reason:

"Dog owners have been urged by the Greater St. Louis Veterinary Medical Association to provide bird houses for purple martins because, by eating mosquitoes, the birds help to keep dogs healthy.

"In one day, a purple martin can eat 2,000 or more mosquitoes, which are believed to be the most common carrier of the parasite causing heartworm infection in dogs. Mosquito control, and treatment of infected dogs as well, are primary concerns in preventing the spread of the parasite, it was noted. . . ."

The list of such organizations, institutions, and individuals endorsing purple martins and modern martin housing is growing rapidly and includes the prominent and authoritative Grand Rapids, Michigan, Audubon Society, one of the nation's most effective organizations in the promotion of both purple martins and bluebirds.

A recent society newsletter said:

"We are often asked to recommend a purple martin house and since some of our members have experimented with various types of wooden and aluminum houses, the consensus of opinion seems to be in favor of an aluminum house which combines certain features regarded as quite desirable which are not generally found in either wooden or other aluminum houses. The Trio-Musselman house . . . incorporates the features desired. The National Association for the Protection and Propagation of Purple Martins and Bluebirds favors the Trio-Musselman house 'as the standard for design features'."

After four years, favorable opinion of the purple martin seemed almost unanimous.

But not quite.

The martin did not become America's most wanted

bird without overcoming some obstacles. Skeptics occasionally questioned the bird's effectiveness, but none could mount a serious challenge in view of the overwhelming evidence being accumulated that the bird does do a good job of controlling insects as well as being a favorite bird in other respects.

The most serious challenge came from the Houston area in the spring of 1966 when the martin was accused of eating honey bees in great quantities. Joe C. Pouncey, treasurer of the Harris County Beekeepers Association, claimed that the martin was a menace to the bees and that all martin houses should be torn down to protect the bee population.

Allison Sanders of the Houston *Chronicle* relayed Mr. Pouncey's sentiments to the public in the April 29, 1966 issue in an editorial entitled "Bee-Ware the Martin." Sanders wrote:

"There are at least two sides to every question and the truth in this cliché is proved in a letter from Joe C. Pouncey, security officer at the San Jacinto Bank of Pasadena and treasurer of the Harris County Beekeepers Association.

"Until Pouncey's letter arrived I had felt, as most people probably do, that purple martins are as sacrosanct as motherhood and the flag—they eat mosquitoes, so who could be against them?

"Pouncey and the other beekeepers are, to name several.

" 'Who in the world sponsored this hoax of purple martins eating mosquitoes?' Pouncey demands. 'They really are the most predaceous enemy the honey bee has. Why would a martin go to the trouble of hunting mosquitoes when, with no effort at all, he can soar above the approach to a colony of honey bees and pick off the workers coming in so loaded with honey that they can't even take evasive action?

84

" 'Martins feed during the day, while the mosquitoes are safely hidden in the grass and weeds. About the time the mosquitoes come out in the late evening the martins are full of honey bees and heading to their nice apartment complexes, built by unthinking humans who don't realize the importance of the honey bee.'

"If martins and mosquitoes and honey bees wore hats," concluded Sanders, "like in TV westerns, it wouldn't be so hard to tell the bad guys from the good guys."

The Houston *Post* also published Pouncey's comments, and several other newspapers and radio commentators also noticed the comments and relayed them to the public, sometimes accompanied by an unspoken "A*ha!*"

Not everyone agreed with Mr. Pouncey's assessment of the martin and its alleged appetite for bees.

James Audubon wouldn't have agreed. He flatly declared, "These birds seldom seize the honey bee."

William J. Mellor of Eureka Springs, Arkansas, wouldn't have agreed, either. His extensive colonies of both purple martins and honey bees co-exist quite agreeably.

The *Chronicle* and the *Post* were deluged with letters in the martin's defense.

George Mobus of the Griggsville Wild Bird Society identified the real culprit as the bee martin, or eastern kingbird, which does have an appetite for honey bees. It is a member of the flycatcher family, not a swallow. Mobus wrote:

"There is a wild bird species noted for its appetite for honeybees. This bird is unfortunately known by many people as a 'bee martin.' This bird is neither a martin nor any member of the swallow family. It is actually the eastern kingbird, member of the so-called tyrant flycatcher family of birds. The kingbird in color and general configuration (having almost black wings, tail, and upper part, and with a fan-shaped tail) can, by the unacquainted,

85

be easily mistaken for the purple martin, particularly the female of the species. This bird may well be the enemy of beekeepers, but you can be sure it is the friend of every farmer, for it is the undaunted foe of crows, hawks, and many other large predatory birds.

"If the Pasadena bee man quoted in your news story is, indeed, correct in that the birds seen above the bee colonies were purple martins, we can tell him exactly what these martins were doing, and that they were not eating honey bees! There are a number of species of dragonflies. The smaller and lower-flying dragon flies are frequently called 'mosquito hawks.' The larger dragonflies will fly high in the air and the principal food of this type of dragonflies is honeybees! One of the favorite foods of the purple martins is these larger dragonflies, and when the martins see these dragonflies concentrated, they will attack and destroy great numbers of them.

"Thus, they are actually saving the lives of the honeybees, which would, otherwise, be prey to the dragonflies."

Pete Jury of Houston, who has a beehive in his yard, wrote that he resented the articles condemning martins.

"Other people with bees and purple martin houses have never seen the purple martin catch a bee, but instead they go high in the air, dodging here and there, feeding on mosquitoes." said Mr. Jury.

Jim Tom House of Houston referred to Bulletin Number 179 of the United States National Museum, prepared by Arthur Cleveland Bent, and pointed out that the study made by Professor F. E. L. Beal and detailed in that bulletin, said, "To accusations that martins destroy honeybees, he had a definite answer that in only five out of 200 stomachs did honey bees appear, and every one of them was a drone."

Joe F. Combs reported in his column, "Farm Corner," in the Beaumont, Texas *Enterprise,* the experience of

The eastern kingbird, a favorite of many in its own right, has the undesirable characteristic of occasionally eating too many honeybees. It is similar in appearance to the purple martin, and the martin sometimes is confused with it.

B. B. Horn of Vidor, Texas, who had a swarm of bees actually occupying one of the gourds used by martins on his place. Mr. Horn's observations are among the most interesting to be related in the honey bee-purple martin controversy.

" 'There is a male purple martin that belongs in a 25-compartment house about 50 feet away (from the bees) that has the habit of crawling into and resting or sleeping in the gourd next to the one the bees have taken over. I have been watching him now for five days. When he goes into the gourd several bees go over to where he sits with his head out the hole.

" 'When the bees come near he just shakes his head. The bees don't bother him, and he doesn't bother the bees. So if anyone believes purple martins eat honey bees, they are wrong, and I have the proof right here at my place. . . .' "

Mr. Combs concludes, "Maybe the purple martin is being accused of something he is innocent of. If bees remain where he is supposed to have eaten them, that doesn't seem to add up, does it? If the bees stay, they certainly have not been eaten."

Honey bees do have numerous natural enemies, including skunks, bears, kingbirds, dragonflies, robber flies, praying mantises, spiders, and toads, to name a few, but the martin is not among them.

After five years of testing, martins reveal no negative characteristic any more serious than their chatter in the early morning hours.

Their resultant popularity has spread so rapidly, in fact, that it has reached as far away as the South Pacific, making them more than just America's "most wanted bird."

Tahiti, in the lush, tropical beauty of the Society Islands near New Zealand, abounds in all sorts of chattering, colorful birds, some of which defy description. Although they are very decorative, they're not the birds Tahitians feel they need most, apparently.

The islanders have studied the possibility of bringing purple martins to that area in order to improve control of disease-carrying insects.

William Albert Robinson of Papeete, capital of Tahiti, contacted Dr. T. E. Musselman in Quincy to ask his opinion on the possibility of "transplanting" martins. Robinson is concerned with Tahiti's filariasis control and research program. Filariasis is a disease caused by nematodes—mosquito-borne parasites that lodge in the blood or tissues.

Dr. Musselman advised Robinson that the feasibility of transporting adult martins was unknown but the shipment of adult birds might be impossible because of the martin's exclusive diet of flying insects. He stated, however, that the transportation of both adult martins and martin eggs could be tried, if the islands decided it was feasible to give the bird a try.

The Griggsville Wild Bird Society welcomes inquiries of this nature from other lands and has offered its assistance in conducting any tests necessary to determine the suitability of these birds for other areas.

Tahiti was not the only Pacific island group to exhibit curiosity about the bird. Hawaii, the Union's beautiful 50th state, which lies like a string of jewels in the Pacific Ocean, has shown keen interest in purple martins.

In an article in the Honolulu *Star Bulletin* in 1965, Ligaya Fruto refers to the martin as "among the world's most useful birds," and asks, "Is this purple bug-eater the answer to Hawaii's prayer?"

Fruto writes, "Attention Hawaii bird lovers, fruit growers, insect haters:

"There could be purple martins in your future.

"These birds that bird books described as 'most beneficial' could be imported to Hawaii to rid this land of year-long summer insect pests that annoy tourists and islanders alike.

"Jack L. Throp, director of the Honolulu Zoo, said that he would be happy to give the first batch of purple martin immigrants a cool and care-free home in the Zoo."

Another question involved in the introduction of this species to Pacific islands is that of migration. No one is certain that, if successfully transported, the birds would then make their annual migratory trip to Brazil or return to the islands. Throp reasoned, "They are homing birds. You might be able to keep them if you move their homes with them. Otherwise, they might go back to wherever they came from."

"As far as I can find," said Throp, "the martin is a highly desirable bird. We've had some birds that eat fruit, but the martins wouldn't destroy fruit. They might even help with the fruit fly, flying ants or termites, beetles, mosquitoes. They eat all these."

As there was no objection from the state's fish and game division, Throp and other interested parties decided to give the proposal extensive study.

More recently, the island of Jamaica has shown interest in encouraging martins for insect control. Jamaica, in the center of the Caribbean Sea south of Cuba, lies near the martins' migration route. The possibility of inducing martins to nest there is being studied.

CHAPTER VII
THE COUNTRY MARTIN:
HIS DAYS ON THE FARM

There is little resemblance between the modern mechanized farms of today and the crude grain fields of those earliest American farmers, the Indians. But through the years all farmers, whether tilling the soil with giant diesel-powered equipment or with primitive wooden hoes, have found themselves doing battle with common foes—insect pests and predatory birds.

The Choctaw and Chickasaw Indians were perhaps the first Americans to deliberately set about controlling these pests. When the first white men arrived on this continent, they discovered that the Indians were attracting colonies of purple martins to their villages. The earliest white settlers—especially the farmers—quickly adapted this same effective and low-cost means of fighting the pests. As the population grew and spread over the country, martin boxes and gourds were very much a part of the rural American scene.

To the modern farmer, faced with the problem of increasing production while reducing operating costs, a colony of purple martins on his place can be of considerable value. A single martin can eat 400 flies in one day. A colony of 24 martin families thus could destroy nearly two million flies each month!

Mr. and Mrs. Curtis Hodson, who live near Coatesville, in Hendricks County, Indiana, have built more than 100 martin houses and have erected many of them on their own farm, where they raise cattle. They say the martins keep down both flies and mosquitoes and are worth many dollars in profit to their operation annually.

That sentiment is echoed by the Wilbur Hall family of Cowden, Illinois. The Halls have nearly a dozen martin houses around their home northeast of Cowden and annually host an average of 70 pairs of martins. All of the Hall family enjoys the activities of the birds as they sweep across the yards and adjacent fields, and the Halls feel certain that the notable absence of mosquitoes at their farm is due to the birds.

Stockmen and dairy farmers know well the profit losses caused by insects that do no more than just irritate the animals. These pests retard the growth rate of calves, they prevent proper weight gain of cattle on feed, and they reduce milk production in dairy herds. Bots, anthrax, anaplasmosis, encephalitis, poultry tapeworm, and other fly-carried diseases add staggering amounts to the total farm losses.

To comprehend more fully the economic potential of martins on the farm, let us take the number of martin houses handled by MoorMan's in its remarkable one-month sale in February of 1966. When installed on farms throughout the country and fully inhabited with a pair of martins in each compartment and starting with May 1, with each pair raising four fledglings and departing for Brazil on August 15, this would mean that their departure would leave us with 144,013,060,000 fewer mosquitoes to swat, or 28,802,012,000 fewer flies for the cows to swish off their backs with their tails.

Or, again, if we were to take six flies on the average for each swish of a cow's tail, this would be 4,800,435,332 swishes during this same period, or a lot of wasted energy. Now if we were to compute that one swish of the tail takes as much energy as one step, and each step is equal to one foot, a cow would walk 909,170 miles, or around the world more than 36 times on this tail-swishing energy.

One final calculation: With martins needing their weight

Curtis Hodson of Coatesville, Indiana, has no way of calculating exactly what the martins mean to his cattle operation in terms of dollars and cents. But Mr. Hodson is certain they more than repay any effort made in their behalf, by keeping his stockyards free of insects that otherwise would irritate the cattle and retard gains.

in insects each day to survive, and with the male weighing four ounces, the female three ounces—and assuming the fledglings were of equally distributed sexes—using these weights and heavy dump trucks, with each truck hauling one ton of these bulky insects, it would require 7,896 truck loads to feed this army of martins during their summer stay on these farms.

These little exercises in mathematics illustrate the important economic factor these birds can be.

Early in this century, a Georgia peach grower set up rows of martin houses in his orchard. As a result, the curculio beetle that caused millions of dollars in damage

93

to fruits elsewhere in the area was practically unknown in his orchard.

More recently, martins are being used successfully in mango groves in Florida. "Sarge" O'Neill, the noted cartoonist who has been a martin booster for 40 years, recently wrote:

"The purple martins are considered almost a patron saint by the mango fruit growers here in the Miami area. We people who have mango trees are deeply indebted to the purple martins for protecting our trees from the dreaded Mediterranean fruit fly. Our records show that the fruit fly has never been found in the area where purple martins abide. They are the best insurance a mango grower can have, saving him thousands of dollars. The Mediterranean fly can wipe out an orchard in no time."

This year, fruit growers in Griggsville are preparing to sell for the first time, "Purple Martin Apples," grown with the use of a minumum of insecticides and consequently certain to be more healthful to the consumer.

Organic Gardening and Farming magazine reported in its February, 1965, issue that a Washington state forester is attempting to build up the bird population in that state's woodlands to eliminate the need for much poison spraying. The editorial writer pointed out that a single swallow family eats about 300,000 forest insect pests each season.

In recent decades many busy farmers have had to do without the benefits provided by these birds. The problems posed by the installation and maintenance of the old-style, heavy, bulky wooden houses were just too great. Such houses had to be taken down and stored each fall and had to be repainted frequently to keep them acceptable to the martins. Then, too, the houses were almost impossible to keep free of sparrows and starlings. The farmers had little time during the busy spring weeks to climb up to the martin houses every few days in order to remove the nesting materials of these pest birds.

All of these problems have been solved by the recent introduction of lightweight aluminum houses. Little or no maintenance is required. Starlings will not inhabit them, and their lightness and ease of access makes discouragement of sparrows a quick and simple process. Being cooler and freer of parasites, they aid the survival of more young birds and thereby build up the effectiveness of the farmer's colony more rapidly.

Each martin house should be installed in an open area, at least 25 feet away from buildings or branches of trees. A height of 8 to 15 feet is satisfactory. Houses may be installed anywhere that they will not interfere with traffic of animals or machines. Those at the Hodson farm in Indiana are installed in the open areas of feed lots. If they are installed in the center of such areas, be

The model 32MPD 8-compartment house has become a familiar part of the American farm scene, as farmers have remembered the confidence their ancestors had in these birds.

certain that the mounting poles are firmly anchored in the ground so that cattle jockeying for position or status in the feedlot do not knock the poles down, disrupting the activities of the martins and their young.

Many of today's farmers will remember that their parents and grandparents had martin houses on their farms years ago. These old-time farmers had neither the time nor the inclination to take all that trouble just to hear the birds sing. All pets had to have some functional value as well as being a friend of the family. Dogs were usually effective as watchdogs or livestock dogs; cats were effective ratters and mousers or they were disposed of. These farmers knew the value of the purple martin and considered colonies of these birds to be very real assets to their farming operations.

Holiday Inn central in Houston reflects America's enthusiasm for the annual spring arrivals of "man's best summer friend."

A new symbol of the widespread interest in purple martins is the
40-ft. tall martin tower (right) in Griggsville, "The Purple Martin
Capital of the Nation," but Griggsville was not the first community to discover the benefits of these birds. Greencastle,
Pennsylvania (above) has respected and enjoyed the martins
since 1840, and has maintained multi-compartment houses for
them in the business district. Note houses on utility poles at
right and left in above photo.

98

New worlds are opening up for the martins as people find new ways to enjoy their benefits. These martins help keep the Sears Garden Center in Quincy, Illinois, bug free.

While purple martins soaring through the sky in Griggsville have new modern houses to which to return, our beneficial ground feeding birds are benefiting, too, from the interest aroused by the martins. The Cardinal Garden, which has 1,016 sunflower-shaped feeders and requires more than a half-ton of seed to fill completely, was dedicated in 1965. Doing the honors were Joe Ackles, chairman of the park board; J. R. Skinner, manager of the Western Illinois Fair; and three Boy Scouts, who volunteered to keep feed in the feeders. They are (left to right) Ricky Allen, Ricky Phillips, and Freddie Slight.

103

Martins live in luxury in this purple martin castle, which can be purchased in 24- or 36-compartment sizes and with a crank for raising and lowering.

Martins sometimes bring home sticks a little too big for their nests. The following pages give more insight into the living habits of this fascinating feathered friend of man.

Martin above succeeded in picking up a stick more than two feet long, but did not succeed in getting it into his nest. Two martins at left were photographed picking up "mortar" in a patch of muddy earth, one of infrequent times when martins can be seen on the ground.

Contrast between nests of house sparrow and purple martin can be seen in above photo. Sparrows fill their cavities with a loosely-assembled mass of miscellaneous items. Martin nest is low, compact, and has a rim of mud on the edge next to the entrance hole. Lower photo shows martin nest freshly lined with green leaves and with eggs in nest. Female martin lays an average of five eggs per season.

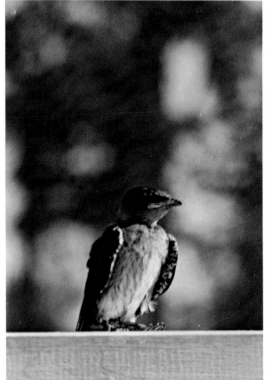

Feeding occupies a large amount of time around a martin colony during the approximate month before fledglings leave the nest. When the young leave the nest they are at first cautious, unsure of themselves, and rest often, but they learn rapidly and soon are flying with all the skill of the older birds.

Martins perform many normal activities on the wing, including drinking and bathing. Martin moving toward right in this photo was skimming just above the water and had just left ripples behind it where its beak flicked the surface for a few drops of water. (On rare occasions when martins feed young birds on the ground, they will do this, too, without landing.) Below a martin is shown getting green leaves for its nest, one of the few occasions when a martin will land in a tree during the early part of its nesting season. However trees often are used as assembly area roosts later in season.

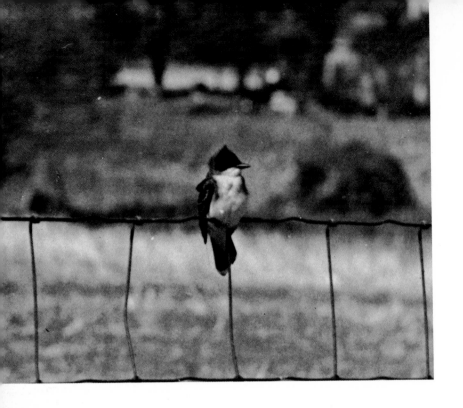

The eastern kingbird, sometimes called the "bee martin" and often mistaken for a martin, is shown above in a typical setting. This bird may sit for hours on the same fence or reed, occasionally darting out to snatch a passing insect, and then returning to the same spot to perch. Crevices in brick wall at right illustrate ideal nesting situations for the house sparrow and starling. In photo at top a sparrow (left) and starling are shown investigating the two crevices. In center photo the starling emerges from lower crevice. In lower photo the starling flies away from the wall, possibly to tell its friends about this beautiful home site.

110

PART II
WHAT YOU SHOULD KNOW ABOUT
THE PURPLE MARTIN

CHAPTER VIII
THE PURPLE MARTIN TIMETABLE

The annual arrival and departure of the purple martin highlights each year for the martin enthusiast. The explanation for the birds' particular timetable still is a question that fascinates ornithologists and naturalists.

THE MARTINS ARRIVE

Bird enthusiasts who host purple martins wait anxiously for their birds to arrive in the spring. The appearance of the first scout is a moment of excitement, and the first arrivals of the main flock are cause for elation.

Until the birds' departure at summer's end, martin hosts are keenly aware of the daily activities of their guests and the progress of the young birds. Many keep thorough records of arrival and departure dates, the number of young raised, the assembly area used in late summer, and other pertinent information.

Some are able to band their birds and keep continuing records on the same individual members of their flock.

As might be supposed, those flocks breeding in the south reach their grounds earlier than those breeding farther north. The appearance of martin scouts begins in late January in Florida and extends through April as the birds wing their way into the northernmost states and Canada.

The scouts are older males, whose job it is to determine the existing food supply and housing in an area and to bring in the main flocks when the area is able to support them. Sometimes scouts will make several trips into an area before determining that conditions are satisfactory.

Usually they are correct in their assessments, but sometimes they are not. Occasionally, as in 1966, whole flocks will move into an area for a time and then move back to the south as cold weather cuts down the insect supply in their chosen locale.

Sometimes, as also happened in 1966, cold weather will descend so rapidly that the birds are unable to retreat before it, or they already have begun to nest and will not leave their homes. In these cases, the absence of flying insects causes the starvation of great numbers of the birds.

After the scouts come the flocks of more mature birds, with the younger birds following later. Males usually precede females in these migrations. In some instances, the females lag behind by as much as two weeks.

The birds do not nest immediately but seem to enjoy the spring weather flying about and gossiping. Nesting often begins as late as June, but when it does begin, the martins go about it in earnest. Because of the wide range in nesting times, martin houses can be erected as late as June in the northern states and still attract occupants. However, it is best to put them up when the first scouts are due in the area.

The Griggsville Wild Bird Society has received reports of arrivals and departures from observers throughout

The closing of houses in winter (as here, with an aluminum plug) is important to prevent house sparrows from becoming firmly entrenched while the martins are away. Many wooden houses must be taken down and stored in winter.

Three cold birds are shown huddled on a house during the first cold snap which hit Griggsville in the spring of 1966. The city had no martin fatalities, but there were fewer martins than during any season of the four-year history of the project. Other martins which normally would have made Griggsville their home apparently stayed in the south. The house shown here is one of those used for various experiments and is equipped with trapping compartments. Cords on end of house trigger drop panels which close all 12 compartments simultaneously.

the nation. Arrival dates from a given area often will be contradictory, which leads the society to conclude that the scouts can be present in a vicinity for several days without being noticed. Nevertheless, the society encourages all observers to submit arrival and departure dates annually, feeling that over the course of several years, errors will tend to compensate for each other and establish reliable average arrival dates for all areas.

Departure dates submitted to the society are considered more accurate. If a colony of several dozen purple martins headquarters in one's yard all summer, it is quite obvious when their cheerful, bubbling chatter is suddenly missing.

The arrival and departure dates for the past four years in Griggsville, where a large percentage of the population watches for the birds, show a great regularity:

    1963: March 17–August 19
    1964: March 11–August 15
    1965: March 17–August 16
    1966: March 14–August 16

117

Following are some early and late arrival and departure dates representing extremes and not typical dates. Martins are rarely found this early or late in these areas.

Nova Scotia, Canada: April 15–September 15
Ontario, Canada: March 15–September 15
Alberta, Canada: May 1–September 1
Massachusetts: April 1–September 15
Pennsylvania: March 15–October 1
North Carolina: March 1–October 1
Florida: February 1–November 1
Louisiana: February 1–October 15
Tennessee: March 1–October 1
Ohio: March 15–October 1
Illinois: March 1–September 15
Arkansas: February 15–October 1
Texas: February 1–October 15
Colorado: April 1–September 1
North Dakota: April 15–September 1
Washington: April 15–September 15
Arizona: April 1–September 15

THE MARTINS DEPART

Summer's end brings a sad moment to martin hosts. Suddenly the air is no longer filled with their friendly chatter, and despite the presence of other song and garden birds, the atmosphere seems strangely empty and quiet for several weeks after the martins leave.

When the young birds learn to fly, their parents take them on ever-lengthening training flights in preparation for their exodus. In late summer in the northern states and from mid-summer through autumn in the southern states the birds begin to congregate in assembly areas, usually beside large bodies of water or in swampy areas.

One can readily understand why such areas are preferred, if one remembers that the individual martin daily

118

Small flocks perched on television antennas herald the approaching departure of the birds—usually a month before. These small groups form into progressively larger flocks along rivers, lakes, and swamps until the time comes for the flight south.

requires its own weight in flying insects. A flock of 10,000 purple martins averaging 3½ ounces apiece requires nearly that same weight—a total of almost 2,200 pounds or more than a ton—of flying insects each day. Swampy lowlands normally are the only areas that can produce such a quantity, even for the short period the flocks are present preparing for their southward journey.

The martins return to their house and home grounds for part of each day, but they spend their nights and progressively more time each day associating with the birds in their assembly area.

Although many birds are feeding at all times in the vicinity of these assembly areas, many more of them—sometimes numbering well into the thousands—perch in trees or on wires. Occasionally, as if on an unspoken signal, hundreds of them leave their perches simultaneously and swarm away for a short tour of the area and then return to their perches.

The martins' departure for the south from a general area may extend over a period of weeks. Large flocks leave at intervals of several days. This is nature's way of assuring them enough food along their journey and of preventing the entire bird population of a particular area from being lost in a single storm.

Among martin enthusiasts, assembly areas are well known. Those at the Ohio State Penitentiary in Columbus and at Chicago's Montrose Harbor attracted considerable attention in 1966. At the penitentiary, near the juncture of the Scioto and Olentangy Rivers, martins have congregated for many years. The flock that gathered there in August numbered more than 13,000, according to Warden Ernie Maxwell, who has been interested in the birds for years.

The Montrose Harbor flock has not been as consistent as the Ohio flock in its behavior, according to Dr. William Beecher. "Twenty years ago they held their flights near Evanston," he said. "Then they moved over to the Fullerton Beach area. Now they're at Montrose."

Most of the nation's rivers and major lakes undoubtedly have assembly areas at intervals along their shorelines. To our knowledge, no agency has kept a comprehensive record of these areas or made an extensive study of their shifts over the years.

The Griggsville Wild Bird Society has undertaken such

120

This martin flock, shown here in a 1962 Chicago Tribune photo, was spotted near Lake Michigan on Chicago's north side. Note guy wires barely visible in background, which are also covered with martins.

121

a study and welcomes data on locations, populations, and departure dates of assembly area flocks.

National Museum Bulletin No. 179 contains some interesting observations of martin flocks in earlier times. The bulletin states:

"Another trait of the martin that has long attracted attention and produced much writing is its communal roosting habit late in summer, when the species gathers in great flocks preparatory to and during migration. Concentrations up to 100,000 birds have been noted, and the attendant noise sometimes results in such a nuisance to people that direct efforts are made against the birds and many killed in various methods. To some degree these roosts are a parallel to those of the vanished passenger pigeon in that branches of trees are broken by the weight of the birds and, as Arthur T. Wayne (1910) puts it, the noise produced by such a multitude resembled the sound of escaping steam. In 1905 a huge roost at Wrightsville Beach (near Wilmington), N. C. was attacked by irate citizens and 8,000 to 15,000 birds were killed. The North Carolina Audubon Society succeeded in convicting 12 of the offenders, who were fined.

"G. Clyde Fisher (1907) describes a roost near Quincy, Fla., which he estimated to contain 5,000 birds and, like Wayne, was impressed with the noise, which he also described as being 'much like escaping steam.'

"A typical roost, and a very well known one, was that at Cape May, N. J., written of in detail by Witmer Stone (1937). Students should peruse his account with great interest. It is too long to quote here, and since 1936 the roost has been deserted not only by martins but by robins, starlings, and grackles. However, it may sometime again be instituted, and extracts of Stone's account are given herewith:

" 'For many years it (the roost) was located on the

122

Physick property on the principal street of the town. Here there is a grove of silver maples about thirty feet in height and covering an area of some two acres, growing so close together that their tops join one another, making a dense canopy with constant shade. * * * Were it not for this roost, the only one in South Jersey so far as I know, martin history at Cape May would come to a close early in August when the last of the fledglings become self dependent and sail away with their parents. But as it is, though there may be days in August when practically no martins are to be found for miles around Cape May from sunrise to sunset, they will gather in ever increasing numbers to pass the night in this small grove which, so far as our eyes can detect, offers no advantages over hundreds of similar groves past which the birds must have flown.' "

THE MYSTERY OF MIGRATION

One of the great unexplained mysteries of the world is the exact method by which martins from throughout the North American continent fly thousands of miles to Brazil each year and then, a few months later, find their way back—most of them to the same neighborhoods in which they nested the previous year.

During the winter months, the martins concentrate chiefly in the Amazon Valley of Brazil (Manaqueri, Barra do Rio Negro, and Itaituba). They also have been found in the coastal regions of Brazil (San Luiz, Rosario, Rio de Janeiro, and Iguape).

Throughout the migration period and the winter stay in Brazil, they are primarily free-flying. They do not nest in the southern hemisphere. There are members of the swallow family that nest in the southern hemisphere, but the martin is not among them. They feed in the air, of course, and roost in protected places, on tree

123

branches and on weeds in marshy areas. Sometimes they roost in great concentrations—several thousand birds within a small area—and in such areas they practically eliminate all flying insects.

These concentrations undoubtedly are similar to the flocks that congregate in assembly areas in the northern hemisphere and, in fact, may be the same flocks.

Brazilians are not so keenly aware of the martins as are the people of the northern hemisphere. This is so for two reasons. First, martins inhabit principally those parts of Brazil having a very small percentage of the human population—the moist jungle areas in the Amazon Valley. Second, as martins do not nest in Brazil, martin houses are useless in attracting martins to an individual's home.

Brazilians undoubtedly are aware of the birds' insect-eating capabilities, however, and appreciate their presence even for a relatively short period each year.

Authorities disagree on the routes used by purple martins in migrating from Brazil to North America, as conclusive information is not yet available. Do the birds use the Mexico land route used by the cliff swallow? Do they follow land through Central America and then island-hop from Yucatan to Cuba to Florida? Do they use the "Bobolink route," making the long haul from South America to Jamaica and then island-hopping on into Florida? Do they use the eastern route, island-hopping around the eastern end of the Caribbean, through the West Indies and into Florida?

Some authorities feel they could not use the "Bobolink route" because of the long flight from the South American coast to Jamaica and the martins' habit of flying only during the day.

It is my belief that martins use several routes, including the Mexican, "Bobolink," and eastern Caribbean routes.

Progne subis subis

Progne subis hesperia

The western martin, sometimes designated as Progne subis hesperia, follows a migratory route through central America. Other martins are assumed to use both the Jamaican "bobolink route" (center of map) and the eastern Caribbean island-hopping route.

We are sure that at least one of the water routes is used, because Florida is the first state to host martins each year. We think it quite probable that the long water route is used by at least some of the martins, as some ship captains have reported sighting what they believed to be martins over the middle of the Caribbean. This route involves approximately 500 miles of open water, but this is within the martins' capabilities under favorable conditions.

In Doppler radar speed tests made in 1963 and 1964 at the University of Michigan biological station, Gary Schnell gauged martin speeds on windless days in a range up to 41 miles per hour. Aided by warm southern air currents, flight speeds up to 60 miles per hour are conceivable. This would put the "Bobolink" route through Jamaica well within the capabilities of the martins.

The full extent of the martins' migratory pattern isn't quite as well-known as that of many other birds, including other members of the swallow family, but we hope to have these facts well-defined within the next few years.

Arrival of the martin scouts is fairly punctual each year, but the arrival of the flocks depends upon general weather conditions. As mentioned earlier, it is the responsibility of the scouts to determine adequacy of food supplies and available housing and to bring the flocks into an area only when it will support them.

But where are the flocks while the first scouts are entering the country each year? Must the scouts fly all the way back to South America to report on northern conditions, or just back to islands in the Caribbean or the tropical areas of central America? The role of the scout is probably not as vital in the coastal areas as it is in bringing the flocks from the coastal areas northward.

Much remains unknown about martins, but thanks to the renewed national interest in the bird and to the work

126

of the Griggsville Wild Bird Society, more is known about the species than ever before.

Lack of knowledge about the general aspects of migration applies not only to martins but to all migratory birds. There is very little provable information on the process of migration of any species of bird.

Several theories about the reasons for bird migratory habits are currently being studied.

The mysteries of migration involve both the why and the how. The major theories as to why birds migrate include the northern and southern ancestral home theories, the continental drift theory, and the theory of photoperiodism. In brief, these are as follows:

The northern ancestral home theory contends that all of the northern areas were tropical at some period in history and that birds flourished uniformly throughout the area. As the great ice cap descended over the continent, it drove the birds south ahead of it. As the ice cap receded, the birds attempted to follow it northward into their ancestral homes, but with each winter they are driven south again.

The theory of southern ancestry holds that all birds originated in the tropical central areas and that the overflow from these areas caused the northern areas to be populated, but that many of these birds still must return to the tropical areas during the colder parts of the year.

The theory of continental drift holds that the northern and southern land masses originally were one but drifted into segments. The separation gradually developed the long migratory routes as extensions of age-old flight patterns that originally may have been much shorter.

The theory of photoperiodism holds that migration is induced by the length of the day and the quantity of light to which the bird is exposed each day, and that birds move southward in response to the shortening of the day.

127

All of these theories are widely discussed, but none is universally endorsed. Each contains too many contradictions.

The question of how the birds find their way along routes covering thousands of miles over the curvature of the earth's surface is also widely discussed.

It is commonly believed that ground-feeding birds whose migratory flights take place at night find their unerring way by using a form of celestial navigation.

Dr. William Beecher has made an extensive study of bird migratory habits and subscribes to both the theories of celestial navigation and that length of daylight hours triggers migratory movements. In a recent discussion on general aspects of migration, he said:

"When the endocrine system of a migratory bird has been activated by the increasing hours of daylight in spring, he must go! If you confine him in a cage, then all night, while his wild brothers are migrating overhead, he will face the proper direction, as if in a trance, and flutter his wings!

"My friend, Franz Sauer, the German ornithologist, devised a cage in which captive European warblers could see only the star-filled night sky and showed that they are able to navigate by the stars. This was double-checked by bringing them inside a planetarium in which the orientation of the starlit sky could be changed at will. Radar seems to show that migrants become bewildered in overcasts, but we do not know whether this confusion is due to the absence of stars or the presence of city lights, man's greatest contribution to migration hazards."

Light from certain stars—and perhaps the moon—impinging on the sight sensors at certain angles could guide these birds on an accurate course to their destinations. Light from the sun may be used similarly by daytime-flying birds like the purple martin.

128

This could explain an apparent paradox in the training flights of young birds. When the young take off with their parents for the first time, they fly in northerly directions. Why north? Why not fly south and thus acquaint the young birds with the first part of their route or even get a little head start on the advance of inclement weather?

Perhaps they are being "programmed" for the time when they must find their way back to their nesting ground the following spring. Early training flights to the north may imprint upon the senses of these young birds the light pattern which they must follow the next year.

Dr. Beecher believes that migratory patterns, as well as all other knowledge a bird will need for survival, are present in the egg, and that the migratory pattern a bird inherits ". . . is a flight direction; birds carried hundreds of miles to the right or left of the normal route still fly in the same direction, but they do not arrive at the intended goal."

Just as the science of ornithology has not settled upon the condition triggering the spring migration northward, neither has it fathomed why the birds leave the northern breeding range when they do. We do not agree with the theory that the shortened days of late summer provide the stimulus. If this were the case, would they not leave on the same date each year?

Neither can it be a lack of flying insect food, for, in reasonably normal years, there is often an abundant supply well into October. Indeed, these flying insect-eaters are often criticized because they leave just when we need them most!

One year they will make their final departure from the northern states as early as the end of July. Another year will see them remaining until late August or even early September. Why this variation?

It must not be caused by weather conditions at their breeding range, because, as we have mentioned, the birds often leave during warm weather and in times of abundant insect supply.

Can it be that weather conditions to the south influence their decision? At the time of the autumnal equinox, weather in the Caribbean and Gulf of Mexico areas is often in a state of turmoil. Hurricanes are not uncommon and other tropical storms keep the air masses in wildly erratic motion. Perhaps the birds have some as yet unknown sense that warns them of future turbulent conditions.

Perhaps they are aware of some relationship between the upper and lower atmospheres. Do the speed and path of the jet stream herald either autumns of calm weather in the Gulf and Caribbean areas, or do they warn of violent winds and lashing rains? If the latter is the case, then certainly the birds would leave early to avoid being trapped between cold air moving down from the north and tropical disturbances to the south. Under neither condition could they forage enough food to sustain them.

Undoubtedly, the fact that martins begin to migrate over a period of weeks is an age-old behavior pattern that evolved to prevent all of the birds from being wiped out by a single period of bad weather. But the possibility that birds can make adjustments in their annual migration schedule in order to adapt to hemispheric weather conditions is a relatively new idea.

If the birds do have access to some kind of advance knowledge of weather conditions in other areas, it apparently isn't complete enough to save them from occasionally stumbling into unfavorable weather during early arrivals in the north. Although such errors are uncommon, they occur often enough that the resulting starvation periods have severely reduced the martin population of some areas.

CHAPTER IX
THE MARTIN'S ENEMIES

Even with man and modern science on its side, the purple martin still must overcome a number of obstacles in order to survive and work its miracles. Among these are pesticides, sparrows and starlings that usurp its nesting sites, inclement weather, and a variety of predators—cats, snakes, raccoons, and even an occasional owl.

We will deal with problems in this chapter. The general subject of pesticides will be examined in greater detail because correspondence from society members indicates a particularly keen interest in this subject. It is acknowledged to be one of the vital issues that propelled the Griggsville story into the national spotlight.

THE PESTICIDE MENACE

In 1963, Rachel Carson's book, *Silent Spring,* alerted the nation to the dangers of its national pesticide policy—or lack of it.

The book outlined undesirable side effects resulting from the use of chemical pesticides—the deaths of large numbers of songbirds, fish, small mammals, beneficial insects, and plants. Miss Carson was, until her death several months later, the most talked-about woman in America.

She alarmed the nation, caused some widespread national soul-searching, and precipitated the first intensive examination of the ramifications of massive pesticide use.

In retrospect, Miss Carson's book has lost the aura of alarm that surrounded it and has settled into perspective as the serious and vital warning that it was.

A year after the book was published, the Quincy, Illinois, *Herald-Whig* commented editorially, "There was irony in the fact that the recent death of Rachel Carson, whose book, 'Silent Spring,' a year ago focused attention upon the dangers involved for man and beast in careless use of chemical pesticides, just about coincided with hearings in Washington that began to prove her point.

"At the hearings it was testified that study has determined that millions of fish—including hardy catfish—have been killed in the lower Mississippi River by minute amounts of chlorinated hydrocarbon insecticides."

The fish kill, which numbered approximately 275,000 in both 1961 and 1962 and increased to more than five million in 1963, was attributed principally to Endrin, a chemical previously certified by the United States Department of Agriculture as harmful to insects but, when properly used, not harmful to animals or man.

However, Dr. Donald Mount, a Public Health Service water pollution specialist, testified in 1964 before a Senate committee that three drops of Endrin in the Potomac River would kill all the fish in that river. A million pounds of Endrin per year had been spread over the states of Arkansas, Louisiana, and Mississippi, and this 'proper' use of the chemical was resulting in the deaths of millions of fish.

Despite Miss Carson's warning and the seemingly universal concern for the danger, corrective action was slow in coming. Evidence continued to pile up that the pesticide menace was every bit as serious as *Silent Spring* had outlined and that the effects of chemical residues in natural 'food chains' was becoming more insidious every day.

Marion Sorenson wrote in the *Christian Science Monitor:*

"While the arguments between users of pesticides and the critics of pesticides continue, research being quietly done in the background continues to bring forth disquieting results. Of greatest concern to researchers is the now established fact that some of the longlasting insecticides based on hydrocarbons have become integral parts of some food chains.

"The latest discovery is that penguins and seals in the Antarctic—thousands of miles from any known use of insecticides—have measurable amounts of DDT in their bodies. These animals spend their entire lives in the Antarctic feeding mainly on shrimp and occasionally fish.

"This latest finding indicates that even in the most remote areas DDT has entered the aquatic food chain. The beginning of this chain is plankton, the microscopic plants and animals which thrive by the billions in nutrient rich waters. Without plankton there could hardly be a fish in the sea. Marine biologists are increasingly concerned about the possibility of mass poisoning of these animals.

"Food chains in aquatic environments are particularly vulnerable to the intrusion of these poisonous chemicals. Pesticides washing off sprayed lands enter rivers and streams in very dilute quantities. But marine organisms often concentrate the poison many times. . . .

"Small fish also concentrate pesticides and pass it on to larger fish which eat them. When the larger fish is eaten by a fish-eating bird such as the osprey or bald eagle, the bird gets a concentrated dose of poison.

"The osprey and eagle stand at the top of this kind of marine food chain. And both of these birds are now in biological trouble and are threatened with extinction. The osprey, which used to breed by the hundreds on the east coast, is now down to a few dozen."

The osprey in particular has caused such concern that birding groups in Wisconsin and Minnesota have initiated osprey-nesting success surveys. They report

133

Two of the most outstanding examples of elaborate martin houses are shown here. That at the left is at the home of Capt. and Mrs. Clarence T. Evans of 405 W. Bougainville, Lehigh Acres, Florida. It is a replica of the First Methodist Church of Bonifay, Florida, has 48 compartments, and is insured for $500. At right, shown sitting on its concrete mounting pole foundation, is the large windmill-style house which Charles Butler of Arkansas City, Kansas, replaced with aluminum houses in 1966.

that the results are not very promising. A survey in Michigan showed the same problem: only 20 per cent nesting success among 50 osprey nests surveyed.

Surveys such as these have led officials to believe that chemical residues are affecting the reproductive capacities of the existing birds, and that this may be even more serious than the actual number of birds killed by pesticides.

The plight of the bald eagle has received even more publicity than that of the osprey. In 1963, of 56 specimens found dead or incapacitated in 20 states and two Canadian provinces, all but one (that one was from Alaska) contained DDT. Of five infertile eagle eggs tested, all contained DDT.

It is immediately apparent that any discussion of the menace of indiscriminately-used pesticides must range far afield from the exclusive subject of purple martins. This is because the subject is one that affects the entire balance of nature and the interdependence of all creatures upon each other.

The martin cannot escape the pesticide menace until all other wild animals are reasonably safe from it. Its harmful effects on robins, eagles, ospreys and herring gulls have been more widely publicized, but martins have also suffered. The Griggsville Wild Bird Society has received letters from martin enthusiasts in many states describing losses that cannot be attributed to any of the other common dangers threatening martins.

Typical reports read, "In perfectly fine weather, the birds just start dying. Several of the birds in my colony were dead in their compartments, and several more fell to the ground and died." "These birds experienced tremors before dying and they must be poisoned." "We lost about half our colony last year after the city sprayed for Dutch elm disease; they didn't spray this year and we haven't lost a single bird."

135

In a majority of cases, the bird lovers do not have the dead birds analyzed. Sometimes they do, however, and at least in those cases reported to the society, chemical residues invariably are found in the birds' tissues. Mr. and Mrs. Jack Houston of East St. Louis, Illinois, found in their yard five martins that had died of poisoning (they had them analyzed) and complained they could find no one who would investigate even the possible origins of the poison. Mrs. Houston said calls to the conservation department, Southern Illinois University, the Audubon Society, and even a department store had all proved futile.

Richard C. Utts of the Niagara Falls *Gazette* investigated the problems of birds in western New York and found several authorities in that area who believe that the *Silent Spring* warning sounded by Rachel Carson was accurate and that the predicted dangers are slowly occurring.

Harold Nogle, a purple martin hobbyist, is among those who believe insecticides have drastically reduced the bird population. "In his years since 1925 on Cayuga Island," wrote Mr. Utts, "he has seen fewer and fewer songbirds. He has seen no hummingbirds, bluebirds or wrens in the last several years. He said there is a poison on the market to treat each type of garden flower."

Dr. Robert Andrle, assistant director of the Buffalo Museum of Science, is more cautious about blaming insecticides but concedes that there is a good probability that the insecticides have reduced the number of birds.

Richard Stephenson of Niagara Falls, chairman of the Conservation Forum of New York and the Nature Conservancy, Western New York, believes, ". . . we'll find the public has been misled; we'll find that Miss Carson was right."

Dr. T. E. Musselman, who has watched with concern

the growing use of pesticides since its beginning in the 1940's, recently recalled the following incident:

"Several years ago, I planned to band the young wrens in eighteen boxes along the Hillcrest summer home area at the Sequanota Club, at Charlevoix, Michigan. A travelling agent of a spraying concern convinced the board of directors at the club grounds that the pine trees were infested with rust and a virus disease and should be sprayed. I warned them against the intrusion but the spraying occurred, and the wind carried the poisonous mist from pines to the deciduous trees and bushes. No doubt hundreds of small birds were affected, as it was the height of the nesting season.

"Thousands of worms and caterpillars hung from the trees with threads, and after wriggling in their death

Deluxe models of modern martin castles now can be obtained equipped with cranks, which facilitate the raising and lowering of the castles for nest cleanout, and make martin care quick and easy.

agonies, were picked up by the busy wren parents and fed to their young. Before the spraying there were about one hundred young wrens about large enough to warrant banding and, of course, their flight was but a few additional days away. Unfortunately, the diet of poisoned bugs reduced their numbers until I could find but three babies which were alive and these were in the last box, the unit farthest away from the spraying activities.

"Yes, over the country there are fewer wrens and because of the kind of food they eat and the susceptibility of these sprites to air sprays, the normal complement of these little songsters is really in danger of being vitally decreased."

The pesticide problem has made itself known in some unusual ways.

Two communities have reported damage by pesticides distributed initially in another region of the nation. These pesticides were not transported by water but by air.

In January, 1965, significant amounts of pesticides distributed in Texas were carried in a dust storm as far as Cincinnati, Ohio. Gladwin Hill of the New York Times Service wrote:

"A red cloud appeared high in the sky over this southern Ohio city at noon January 26. A half-hour later rooftops, automobiles, sidewalks and people were covered with the red dust.

"Subsequent measurements, by the city's department for the control of air pollution, indicated that the fallout amounted to as much as nine tons a square mile—140 tons on Cincinnati and as much as 1800 tons on the four-county metropolitan area.

"The dust had traveled more than 1000 miles from the plains of Texas and Oklahoma in an unusual wind-storm.

"Then the Robert A. Taft Sanitary Engineering Center

reported a new cause for concern. Analysis of the dust indicated that it was 'loaded,' as one of the center's scientists put it, with pesticides and other agricultural chemicals that had been placed on farms in Texas days, weeks, months, possibly years before.

"The concentration of these chemicals was not enough to raise apprehension about the dangers to public health from this one episode.

"But to the scientists and engineers of the Taft Center, which is the Pentagon of the United States Public Health Service's war on contaminants, this new sort of fallout signaled the development of another front in the battle against pollution of the nation's water.

"These agricultural poisons—insecticides, herbicides, fungicides and rodent killers—are chemically designed to maintain their potency indefinitely."

The people of the Fargo-Moorhead area in North Dakota and Minnesota also believe their area has suffered from the effects of insecticides sprayed in southern states, but the manner of the poison's transfer to their area is somewhat different from that to Cincinnati. Authorities there theorized that the widespread deaths of purple martins in their area in 1965 were due to insecticides that the birds had taken into their systems en route from their southern homes. The story is explained in the Fargo *Morning Forum* of June 3, 1965:

"Purple martins—the birds that daily eat their own weight in mosquitoes—are dying in the Fargo-Moorhead area.

"Dr. Myron Andrews of the NDSU Veterinary Science Department believes it is caused by insecticides—not from sprays in this area, but from areas between here and Mexico.

"One man, Frank Bohmer of 51 4th Ave. So., Moorhead, reported that all 33 of the purple martins that came to live in his birdhouses have died.

"Dr. Andrews said that he has had others report from the Fargo-Moorhead area of the birds dying. A member of his staff, he said, saw four dead martins in Detroit Lakes.

"Dr. Andrews checked out three of the dead martins, found chlorinated hydrocarbons in the tissues.

"That means insecticides, he says, including such sprays as DDT, Dieldrin, and Endrin.

" 'But,' he said, 'I feel it could not have come from the small amount of spraying done here.'

"What probably happened, he said, is this:

"The weather here has cut down sharply on the number of flying insects that martins depend upon for their total diet.

"Therefore, the birds have been existing on their stored fat, which contains the chlorinated hydrocarbons. That means the birds must have eaten insects that had been sprayed while they were en route to their summer headquarters here."

Inasmuch as the weather had cut down on the food supply in that area, as the *Forum* pointed out, simple starvation cannot be discounted entirely as a possible cause for some of the deaths, but the presence of the chlorinated hydrocarbons in the martin's tissues nevertheless is ample cause for concern.

Typical of reports in which pesticides are the proven killer is this excerpt from the Allentown, Pennsylvania, *Call:*

"Two highly toxic chemical pesticides have been found in dead birds which fell two weeks ago in Forks Township.

"Laboratory tests made by Delare Associates, bacteriologists and research chemists in Philadelphia, disclosed the presence of heptachlor epoxide and dieldrin in a robin and purple martin.

140

"The dead birds were found in the upper portion of the township after alfalfa weevil spraying was done on adjacent farmlands. Complaints of many dead birds and small game were made following the spraying."

Near Ellsworth, Iowa, in May, 1965, a 36-year-old farmer, Richard Ellwood, was stricken with organiphosphorus insecticide poisoning after about 10 days of corn planting, using a parathion-based insecticide designed to kill corn rootworms. He suffered abdominal cramps, headaches, blurred vision, persistent coughing, and nasal discharge, but his health gradually returned, and he was able to resume his farming operations. He is one of thousands of Americans who have suffered nonfatal cases of insecticide poisoning.

Not all Americans have fared as well. More than 100 deaths each year are caused by such poisoning. One of these, the death of three-year-old Billy Ray Salyers in Wabash, Indiana, on July 14, 1965, caused that community to make a serious re-appraisal of chemical pesticides and eventually to abandon its own fogging program.

Billy Ray's death, which was attributed by the Indiana state toxicologist to acute Chlordane poisoning, occurred after the boy wandered into an area where city workers were spraying a fog to kill mosquitoes.

The Griggsville Wild Bird Society subsequently offered its assistance to the community in improving its natural insect control. Since that time, several officials and interested citizens have corresponded with representatives of the society, indicating continued concern with natural insect control in that area.

Official action, as we noted earlier, has been slow in coming.

In 1963, the President's Science Advisory Committee gave its official recognition to the warnings being sounded. The Chicago *Sun-Times,* in its edition of May 21, 1963, editorialized:

141

"The President's Science Advisory Committee has reported what many suspected to be true—the widespread and sometimes indiscriminate use of chemical pesticides is a dangerous practice.

"The report stated that approximately 105 deaths— half of them children—are attributed each year to the misuse of pesticides. The number of nonfatal poisonings cannot be estimated.

"Some of the deaths, the report says, are caused by carelessness and misuse; others are the result of 'PROGRAMS FOLLOWED EXACTLY AS PLANNED.'

"Bird deaths in some areas have approached 80 per cent where poisons were used to control Dutch elm disease, fire ants or Japanese beetles. In 1954 and again in 1956 the entire year's production of young salmon was nearly wiped out in the Miramichi River in New Brunswick, when DDT was used to control spruce budworm.

"The report of the committee is a vindication of those who have, for many years, inveighed against the dangers that could arrive from the indiscriminate use of synthetic chemicals. Not only is life threatened (in Missouri a farmer sprayed his herd of 180 cattle with what he thought was a tick spray. Actually, he reached for the wrong can and sprayed his herd with another insect spray. All 180 cattle died within minutes.) but the ecological balance of nature is upset.

"There are no adequate controls over the use of these substances at the present time. There is no excuse now for continued legislative dodging to avoid responsibility for controls. The President's committee has made it clear that control legislation is needed immediately."

The cattle misfortune described above was repeated on a somewhat smaller scale in West Virginia in 1966 when another rancher used the wrong spray and killed

142

45 of his cattle. At almost the same time, the community of Argyle, Minnesota, was evacuated after a pilot accidentally sprayed the town with a mixture of Parathion.

Although officials of the Argyle area said that no real danger existed after all because the mixture was found to be a nonlethal two-pound solution instead of a lethal eight-pound solution, any amount of Parathion is too much because of the cumulative effect of this and most other insecticides in the tissues.

Almost as significant is the fact that in many cases the insecticides have not proven effective at the job they were primarily designed to do—at all costs—exterminate nuisance insects.

Insects build up an immunity to pesticides, requiring the development of ever stronger poisons.

Then, too, sprayings are not always well-enough timed to provide more than temporary relief. Repeated sprayings are required in order to provide a reasonable amount of freedom from insects. In the long run, birds suffer more than insects during this program.

Claire Pottorf, writing in the Fort Pierce, Florida, *News-Tribune,* pointed up the ineffectiveness of pesticides:

"Anybody with any hide left at all these days can tell you. Man, we've got mosquitoes!

"You know it, the mosquito control forces know it, even the mosquitoes know it. There are so many clouding the skies that untrammeled skin is at a premium.

"But what to do?

"Well, Director Gene Lemire and his St. Louis County mosquito mashers are foggy from all the scientific slaughter, and there are still more bugs."

The growing controversy in legislative halls and council chambers across the land has inspired moments of humor as well as serious debate.

Alderman S. D. Thorn of Paragould, Arkansas, is one

143

of the more dedicated of that city's aldermen. He is also an admirer of purple martins and other wild birds and knows what they can do for man. When the subject of that city's fogging machine came up recently in council, he announced, with tongue in cheek, that he was "glad the mayor plans to use the rolling mosquito spray rig again this summer, because I have personally seen hundreds of mosquitoes meet their death under the wheels of the machine. And I know if mosquitoes are being run over in my neighborhood, they're being run over in all sections of Paragould!"

Though an official, well-developed national policy has been slow in coming, scattered actions have sometimes been very encouraging.

Secretary of the Interior Stewart Udall, who has been working to alert other federal departments to the dangers of pesticides, has prohibited the use of several of them on the 550 million acres of public land under the control of his department. These include DDT, Chlordane, Dieldrin, and Endrin, all known to concentrate in living organisms. His orders directed that priority be given to non-chemical methods of pest control.

Ohio withdrew from registration the chemicals Aldrin, Endrin, and Dieldrin. In 1962, the state of Iowa passed an extensive ordinance regulating the definition, registration, use, and testing of pesticides, even mentioning certain substances by name.

Other states undoubtedly have taken action against specific chemicals when their dangers have been brought to official attention. Actions taken at state levels, however, obviously are not widespread enough to have much significance on a national scale.

On local levels, citizens of many communities have mounted such stiff opposition to the use of fogging machines that such equipment has been banned. Attention

144

has then inevitably turned toward a thorough study of the local environment and the resources provided by nature for insect control.

Zion, Illinois, is a typical case. The citizens initiated a well-organized and well-documented campaign of public information and protest before the city council, causing the council to rescind a chemical program it had just voted to establish. Axel N. Shuster, one of the opponents of the program and a proponent of natural control said, "We think it is important to call attention to the fact that man's harsh attacks on segments of nature with poisons are at best quite ineffective and often harmful to humans, pets, and other life. At worst, these pesticides can be a real threat to the health and life of whole communities, as was experienced in Argyle, Minnesota."

The city of Wauconda, Illinois, passed in 1966 an ordinance requiring the purchase of a city permit—for a fee of $2—before any type of pesticide could be applied anywhere in the city. While the ordinance does not ban the use of any specific chemicals in the city, it requires each registration to state the place and duration of use, expected date of beginning, brand name of the pesticide to be used, antidote for such pesticide, amount to be used, and rate of application. It also requires warning signs in the area of use and advance notice to area residents.

In 1966, the Public Health Service issued a $59,500 grant to the Midwest Research Institute in Kansas City, authorizing it to develop criteria for the first national monitoring system to measure amounts of pesticides in humans. Ten urban stations will be chosen by the institute to collect human tissues and body fluids for pesticide analysis. Eventually, 135 stations will be established throughout the country.

The same year, Sen. Gaylord Nelson of Wisconsin introduced a bill in Congress to ban the sale of DDT.

Sen. Nelson believes DDT and possibly other pesticides are responsible for the dwindling fish and game supplies not only in Wisconsin but in many other states.

He said that, since DDT's introduction in the 1940's, it has "contaminated the atmosphere, built up in the fat of creatures throughout the world, and killed or reduced the reproductive capacity of entire species of birds, fish, and marine organisms."

Sen. Nelson said DDT's tendency to concentrate in the food chain and cause sub-lethal chronic effects on fish and wildlife is well established. "DDT drifts with the air, flows with the rivers, falls with the rain," he said.

The Senator has access to authoritative studies made by his state. The Wisconsin Conservation Department has completed studies revealing heavy DDT buildup in Wisconsin's birds, wildlife, lakes, and rivers.

Prof. Joseph Hickey, professor of wildlife management at the University of Wisconsin, has said, "The problem of insecticides is a far more complex situation than any of us realized 10 years ago."

Prof. Hickey said that while the effects of insecticides used on crops and in the control of Dutch elm disease still are largely undetermined, experiments at the university showed that in DDT-sprayed areas, the mortality rate of songbirds was in direct proportion to the amount of DDT used.

"When DDT was sprayed in Wisconsin to control Dutch elm disease, the robins disappeared," he said. "I've seen these robins die. I've seen them in DDT tremors."

The United States Forest Service announced it did not plan to use DDT in any of its 1966 insect control programs.

In *The Birds,* a Life Nature Library book, Roger Tory Peterson points out the need for a consistent and sensible national policy concerning both birds and pesticides. In illustrating his point, he refers to the opinions of Dr. Hickey:

"Recently, something like a national policy with respect to birds has been evolving in the U. S., but its outlines are contradictory. Dr. Joseph J. Hickey of the University of Wisconsin points out: 'Without a permit you cannot pick up and take home a car-killed Baltimore oriole but you can usually with impunity cut down a tree with an entire oriole nest full of young. You cannot shoot a snowy egret, but you can drain off a marsh on which a whole colony of egret nestlings may depend for food. You cannot shoot a robin, but you can kill it with pesticides.'

"This inconsistency has become tragically clear since World War II and particularly during the last 10 years, when pesticides have been widely promoted, like wonder drugs, as a panacea for all conceivable insect ills and plant diseases. George Wallace, professor of zoology at Michigan State University, in describing the potential effect of indiscriminate spraying on bird life, went so far as to call it 'worse than deforestation, worse than market gunning, worse than drainage, drought or oil pollution. . . .' If the pest eradication programs are carried out as now projected we shall have been witness within a single decade to a greater extermination of animal life than in all the previous years of man's history."

Art Schumann, writing in the February-March, 1966, issue of the *Badger Sportsman* of Chilton, Wisconsin, described the remarkable insect-eating capabilities of many of our bird species, and added, "Let's give the birds a chance to do what we have so far failed to do. There is no doubt that the majority of birds are more beneficial than injurious and that by increasing their numbers we do ourselves a favor. The trouble is that today we put

147

too little emphasis on the education of one another on just how valuable birds are."

Hope Sawyer Buyukmihci, manager of Adams Unexpected Wildlife Refuge at Newfield, New Jersey, in 1964 wrote to the Philadelphia *Enquirer* in rebuttal to an *Enquirer* reader who had urged "all-out war on mosquitoes and certain types of wildlife, bats, red-wing blackbirds and other pests." Mrs. Buyukmihci wrote:

"This demand for all-out war shows a frantic desire to do away with all life but our own. In the end, of course, the weapon will be turned on ourselves, for we cannot live—and who would want to live?—without the marvelous balance of living things of which we are a part.

"We need to consider carefully the natural checks and balances of nature, many of which have been tampered with, bringing us trouble. Where are the thousands of martin houses which would house hosts of purple martins, delightful birds whose favorite food is mosquitoes? Where are bluebird and tree swallow houses which would bring us song and grace as well as keep mosquitoes under control? Why do we allow shooting of our dwindling wildfowl population, who glean millions of mosquitoes from our waterways. Let us wake up, and get busy on building and cooperating instead of destroying."

Dr. Kenneth S. Hagen, associate entomologist in biological control at the University of California's Berkeley experiment stations, has done considerable research in the use of insects to control other insects. He recently remarked, "We would, of course, prefer to use only biological control. But people today demand clean foods. They don't want any insect damage whatever. Which means they are going to have to have chemicals. Perhaps it would be better to have an aphid or two on a lettuce leaf than the residue of a chemical. As a matter of fact," said Dr. Hagen, "many growers now go along with taking a little damage in order to get away from the use of chemicals that have such a broad spectrum of control. Because, as we are learning to our dismay, these chemicals seem to be creating more problems than they solve."

Recognition is coming from all quarters that we are poisoning our entire environment and that it is becoming increasingly urgent for everyone to take a keen interest in the preservation of the health of the natural system which created us.

All of this poisoning has been an attempt to rid our environment of a few species of insects and weeds. In this process we may, in the words of the Quincy *Herald-Whig,* "be throwing the baby out with the bathwater."

Persons who would not dream of removing a few bricks at random from the foundation of a large building would still pump millions of pounds of poison into the atmosphere in an attempt to remove a few segments of our natural structure.

Those who appreciate any of nature's wild creatures recognize this contradiction and have joined the effort to create a more safe and sane national attitude toward chemical pesticides. In this campaign, purple martin enthusiasts have taken the lead, recognizing that their favorite cannot be entirely safe as long as any species of wildlife is threatened with extinction.

SPARROWS AND STARLINGS

The most important natural enemies of the purple martin are not, strangely enough, animals that prey on the birds themselves but animals that usurp their housing —the house sparrow and the starling.

Martins always have been largely dependent upon others for housing. Even when man was not among the martin's benefactors, it depended on woodpeckers to provide most of its nesting cavities. It is one of many species that have benefitted from the woodpeckers' skill.

But the house sparrow and starling, both imports into America from Europe, have shown such skill at adapting to various nesting conditions that they have usurped nearly every type of housing available to martins. Primitive nesting cavities have been appropriated primarily by the starling, but both species have taken over martin house compartments in large numbers. Although martins usually can compete on even terms for compartments, the fact that sparrows remain in a vicinity all winter when most conventional martin houses are left up and open gives the sparrows several months in which to become firmly entrenched and difficult for martins to oust.

Now, however, man is stepping in to turn the tide. Modern martin houses have eliminated one of these species, the starling, as a competitor and are significantly reducing the competition of the sparrow. Before discussing how modern housing discourages sparrows and starlings, let's take a look at these two birds.

The first starlings were imported into America in 1890 by a group that was determined to introduce here every species of birds mentioned by Shakespeare. Sixty of them were released in New York City's Central Park, and now the nation has countless millions of them from coast to coast.

They are aggressive and usurp nesting sites of many types of birds. They often destroy eggs or throw young birds of other species from their nests. They destroy grain crops valued at millions of dollars annually. They flock in cities and defy every ingenious plan conceived by city fathers to drive them away.

They seem to have no effective natural enemy in this hemisphere, although one may be appearing on the scene—the gourmet. In France and in some parts of America, starlings are eaten as a delicacy, wrapped in bacon, roasted, and served on toast.

Starlings are good flyers but spend a great deal of time on the ground. With their waddling gait, they patrol lawns and parks, using their long yellow beaks to penetrate the matlike material near the ground and grub under it for worms and insects. They rid lawns of some harmful insects and include grasshoppers, white grubs, and Japanese beetles in their diet. Like all birds, they aren't all bad, but the good they do does not negate the fact that starling flocks cause millions of dollars worth of crop loss annually and have greatly reduced the population of beneficial birds like the purple martin.

Starlings throw together a nest of twigs and trash in quite a variety of places, but they prefer dark, dreary cavities. They are commonly found in crevices in the walls of buildings and in wooden martin houses that have been allowed to deteriorate.

For martin lovers, the introduction of the aluminum martin house has eliminated the starling as a problem. In the five years of the purple martin program in Griggsville, starlings have never nested in any of the aluminum houses erected there.

The clean, bright nesting compartments of these houses seem to be entirely outside the range of acceptable sites to starlings, although the bird previously was considered adaptable enough to nest in any type of compartment.

Although the starling remains as much a threat to the ecology of our continent as before, the introduction of modern martin housing is at least eliminating it as a problem for the purple martin.

The campaign to control the sparrow has not been quite so simple or clearcut.

The Griggsville Wild Bird Society receives more comment about the house sparrow than any other single species, with the exception of the martin, of course, and the comments about sparrows are almost always complaints.

The house sparrow may well be America's most unpopular bird. Members complain that it is dirty, parasite-infested, noisy and, worst of all, takes over houses intended for martins, tree swallows, and bluebirds.

The English sparrow, more commonly called the house sparrow, was first imported in 1850 when eight pairs were brought into New York state. Importation continued until 1883. Optimism was high at the time, as bird enthusiasts thought these birds would control cankerworms and provide a cheerful addition to the landscape. Since that time, the house sparrow has spread like the starling over virtually the entire continent and has shown an amazing ability to adapt to a variety of nesting sites and food, with apparently no effective natural enemy.

They are very prolific, each pair raising up to five broods per season. They remain in the neighborhood of their birth year round, and whatever ground they lose to other birds in housing battles during the summer is recovered in winter, when they become firmly established in any available housing.

Although not actually a sparrow but a weaver finch, the house sparrow is the only unpopular bird that carries the "sparrow" designation. Several members of the true sparrow family are very popular and beneficial. These include the chipping sparrow, fox sparrow, lark sparrow, song sparrow, and white-throated sparrow.

Like all sparrows and finches, the house sparrow has a stubby beak, but his markings distinguish him from other members of these families. Bird enthusiasts who plan some sort of action against sparrows should be certain that they have the right bird. The male house sparrow's markings include a black throat, with white on the side of the head and chestnut on the top. His back is brown striped and his lower side gray. The female is a duller color, with no black or chestnut markings.

The house sparrow consumes a number of harmful insects, including termites, and a number of nuisance seeds, like crabgrass seeds, in great quantities when available.

Although the sparrow is less an economic disaster than the starling, it is even more proficient as a competitor for both the food and housing of popular songbirds. No housing has yet been contrived that the aggressive sparrow will not move into if permitted.

Modern martin houses have a number of innovations, however, that make the job of combatting the sparrow much simpler and easier than it was previously.

Sparrows can sometimes be discouraged by repeatedly cleaning out their nesting material as soon as they begin to build. Telescoping steel mounting poles and the lightness of aluminum houses make for easier raising and lowering. Fold out doors on individual compartments make the job of cleaning out a sparrow nest quick and simple.

This can be done while martins are nesting in adjoining compartments. Martins do not object to human activity around their nests, and as soon as a house has been raised back up, the martins will return immediately to their nests with no apparent objection to disruption of their activities.

Discouraging sparrows has been undertaken with varying degrees of success. Some have been successful after just two or three efforts; others have reported their sparrows will never become discouraged.

Charles Butler, who filled 58 of his 60 compartments with martins in 1966, did so by systematically cleaning out any sparrow nesting materials each day. He said this would not have been possible without the afore-

153

mentioned features.

Several novel methods of discouraging sparrows have been tried; three reported to the society as being highly successful involved mice and music.

E. Wilcox of 5310 Wriley Road, Washington, D. C., used a transistor radio to rid his martin house of sparrows. The tiny, one-battery transistor radio was left tuned in to a music station for two days (no nights). The martins apparently liked the music, for they stayed. The sparrows left.

H. G. White or rural Danville, Illinois, installed radio speakers in his 60-compartment martin house and controlled the speakers remotely from his ham radio rig in the basement. "The martins love the music, but it scares the sparrows away," he said.

Mrs. A. C. Parrish of Tulsa, Oklahoma, told us of a gentleman who put a live mouse in his martin house before the arrival of the martins. The mouse scared the sparrows away; they chose to remain elsewhere even after the mouse was removed. He cleaned out the sparrow nests and soon obtained a happy martin colony.

Of course, sparrows can be eliminated by shooting them, but this involves killing birds that do have beneficial as well as annoying, harmful traits. Many bird enthusiasts will prefer measures that simply remove the sparrows' activities to another area.

The latest and most effective method of ridding the house and yard of sparrows without destroying them is the use of a sparrow trap. Several are on the market. These can be affixed to a building, post, or tree, but the most common mount is the martin house pole itself.

Bread is the most usual bait; sparrows find fresh bread very hard to refuse.

The chief advantage of a sparrow trap is that the birds can be taken out into the countryside and released again. Sparrows are non-migratory and tend to stay in the vicinity in which they are released. Consequently, those taken several miles from the home and released will not return.

Other birds caught in the sparrow trap can simply be released. Martins and other air-feeding birds will not enter the trap, of course, not being tempted by any food which is not flying, but wrens, grackles, bluejays, starlings, cardinals, and blackbirds will sometimes be trapped.

Ornithologists and naturalists have stated repeatedly for more than 50 years that these two birds—house sparrows and starlings—are threats to the ecology of our continent. Many feel that, if not exterminated, their numbers should at least be decreased.

There is no doubt that these birds are not only threats to our crops but have significantly reduced the populations of some of our favorite song birds. Very few people want a further decline in the population of the purple martin, bluebird, tree swallow, and flicker.

Modern aluminum housing incorporating the Trio-Musselman innovations has made a significant contribution toward combatting the sparrow's and starling's undesirable effects. The trend is shifting, with man's help, in favor of the songbird, without actual harm to its competitors.

Speckled sparrow egg (left) and white martin egg are easily distinguishable.

155

Perhaps other such means can be found to combat other problems created by these two nuisance birds.

WEATHER TAKES LARGEST TOLL

Over the years, the most dangerous enemy of the martin has been the weather. Although adverse weather conditions do not bother martins often, the weather can take a tremendous toll when it does strike.

Martin losses to the weather are often massive, but few have been as sudden or spectacular as that which occurred about 20 years ago when a storm on Pelee Island struck a flock on its way to Ontario. According to R. H. Hesselbart, the widely-read New York bird columnist, more than 10,000 birds were found dead on the island after the storm.

Weather's largest tolls often spread over a wide area of nesting colonies.

Although martins can, like most birds, stand considerable cold, they cannot exist long without food. Flying insects are virtually non-existent during cold weather. Consequently, sudden cold snaps can cause the starvation of thousands of birds in a single area.

Because of the martins' high metabolism rate, they require large amounts of food daily; two to three days without food can kill a martin.

Generally, seasonal weather changes are gradual enough that martins can move ahead of them without any trouble. Occasionally, however, wide areas of the nation experience erratic weather with frequent sudden changes from very mild to cold temperatures. 1966 was such a year.

A study of that year will reveal what happens to the martin population during such a period and what martin enthusiasts must do in order to insure the rapid expansion of the martin population and its preservation at levels which will provide a marked degree of insect control on an overall national basis.

Martins arrived in the northern states earlier than usual in 1966 because of the early spring. The Griggsville Wild Bird Society received reports of earlier-than-usual sightings of scouts from virtually every part of the country west of the Rockies.

But the weather changed abruptly and so did the nature of the reports. Early arrivals were not faring well.

Some stuck it out. Many returned to the south and came back north after the first siege of bad weather. But the weather changed abruptly several times, and the second and third periods of cold reaped large numbers of fatalities. The last cold snap was well into May.

A "strange plague" which hit martins in the Guilford,

Dilapidated wooden houses are made to order for sparrows and starlings. This one in Mason County, Illinois, was loaded with sparrows in every compartment which was still usable.

Connecticut, area in 1966 was soon diagnosed as starvation caused by unseasonably cold weather.

In the Syracuse, New York, area on May 22, 1966, Benjamin Burtt reported, "Right after the snow a week ago, several people called to tell me that martins were dying. John Smith found four on the ground beneath his martin house in Skaneateles. Of the 25 martins at the R. C. Andersons' near Oneida Lake, 12 were dead.

"The worst kill, though, was in the colonies at Dr. E. Kidd's near Chittenango Station. He has a number of martin houses with a total population of about 300. Beneath the houses alone, 120 were picked up. Many others were scattered through the woods nearby. Some would come out of the house, flap their wings a few times and then glide to the ground, but all died. In a brief visit to the colonies, I saw no more than four alive out of the original 300."

Dr. Burtt continued, "I asked Roberta Seaman of Skaneateles to check some of the martin houses in that area and she found some dead ones. However, the colony in downtown Syracuse at the Canal Museum seems to be getting along alright. Frank Thomson of the museum tells me the colony seems to be thriving. Since it is always warmer downtown, perhaps that accounts for their survival. Perhaps there are some flies and other insects downtown that can serve as food."

At New London, Connecticut, several martins in a colony on Pequot-Sepos Road were hit by cars, a fate not normally befalling purple martins. This, too, was traced to the cold weather.

"What is extraordinary," said Curator Robert Kunz of Pequot-Sepos Wildlife Sanctuary, "is that these birds are nesting on the tar surfaces of the road, a thing I have never seen before. The purple martin is almost exclusively a soaring and perching bird. It's my theory that this cold spring and lack of insects have put them down to a pretty low ebb. They seem to be resting on the road to absorb whatever heat radiates from the blacktop.

"Since they have very weak feet, they cannot get off the ground very fast at all."

Rain can take a toll, too, as pointed out by Mr. Burtt:

"Even in the summertime, a long cold period of rain can kill many young and even some adults. According to an account in a book on New England birds, a rainy spell in June, 1929, nearly wiped out all of the martins in eastern Massachusetts."

One of the most interesting accounts of the effects of cold and rainy weather on martins was written by Kay McCracken and appeared in 1966 in the Corpus Christi, Texas, *Caller*. It indicates that the problem of weather is not exclusively a northern and eastern problem. Excerpts from Kay McCracken's account follow:

"That monsoon we had the first week of May was a boon to some, a bane to others. Among bird people, too. Those who were just out looking—and probably more were out looking this time than ever before—saw, immediately following the downpour, one of the truly fabulous migrations of all times. All sorts of birds, including such rarities as western tanagers at Flour Bluff and bob-o-links at Rockport, were seen.

"But there was another side to the coin. Those who had purple martins just bringing off young, sadly and helplessly watched their colonies weaken and die during the unseasonable rains. Dead and dying birds were picked up soaked, chilled, and starving. None could be saved.

"Disasters occurred all over the area. In Premont two pairs and four young, all of a new colony, died. In Rolling Acres, 40 were dead in one neighborhood.

"Joe Cox on Alice Street and his neighbor, Cecil

159

Springer, on Lamont had built up sizeable colonies over the years, adding more apartments as more tenants applied for them. But in all these years, neither has seen such havoc as this. Their martin houses are empty today.

"Becoming landlord to purple martins takes patience. New houses usually stand empty the first season, one pair may use it the next, three or four the third year. But, after that, the colony 'snowballs,' Springer said.

"He had 11 pairs nesting. All 20 rooms in Cox's martin motel were occupied for the first time. (Last year he had 18 pairs, and 16 broods of fledglings.) Ninety per cent of their birds died during the rain, survivors left afterward—as martins will. When families are broken up they quit the disaster area.

"Birds falling into shrubbery and onto the ground alerted them to what was happening. Cox picked up 13, water-logged and lifeless. The first day the dead were males, the second day it was the females. He thinks exhaustion, and perhaps pneumonia, dealt the blow—at least to the males. Since females do most of the brooding, the males were trying to find enough food for both—and some pairs had young to feed as well.

" 'It was just more work than they were up to in such weather,' he surmised. 'Those still in the air in the rain looked heavy, they were soaked. Then the unfed females and young died of starvation, probably the second day.' Females were found dead in the boxes after it was all over.

"Springer rescued six soggy martins from his boxes, dried and warmed them, and forced boiled eggs and crickets into their gapes. But to no avail, they were dead the next day. He thinks starvation wiped out his colony.

"The rain was just too constant. Insects were plentiful, mosquitoes abundant—as everybody knows. One good hour of flying weather each day might have saved them."

Kay McCracken reported that "none could be saved."

160

Benjamin Burtt said, "Unfortunately, there is little man can do to help the martins at such times." R. H. Hesselbart said, "There's nothing we can do. They're just plain starving to death, and there is no way to help them."

In a majority of cases, this has been the result. Yet, cases are on record where adult martins suffering from cold and starvation have been saved by handfeeding. The experience of Mrs. Ramby Rasmussen of Newport, Minnesota, is cited in chapter XIII. In Griggsville, an injured martin was successfully handfed.

The important thing is that it can be done. Satisfactory techniques must be developed for martin enthusiasts to use. A solution to this problem alone will be the greatest boost the purple martin population has ever experienced in the northeast and other parts of the northern states and southern Canada.

Probably the most important factor working for the martin in its efforts to overcome the weather is its speed and flying range. Martins can cover great distances in a day's time and can often retreat south ahead of a rapidly moving cold front.

During periods like the spring of 1966, abnormally large flocks congregate in the south, where martins flourish even in normal times. Their expanded numbers in 1966 can be accounted for by no other explanation than the unseasonably cold weather farther north.

Many of the birds detained in the south by unseasonable weather undoubtedly will return to their northern homes the following season, giving more cause for optimism in the north than might at first be expected when one considers only the relatively small northern population in 1966.

In the Knoxville, Tennessee, *Journal,* J. B. Owen reported in his column, "For the Birds,"

"No one could remember anything like it ever happening

before. After the purple martins had been slow to increase their numbers for a whole month, three people phoned Monday, April 4, to report the spring arrival of martins in unheard-of-numbers." At one location, 88 martins crowded around 34 compartments. At another, 150 martins were counted around 40 gourds.

Owen continued, "Maybe the weather is the answer. The martins have been held back by cold weather. . . . Maybe the flocks were in a sort of traffic jam that piled up when the northbound parade hit the cold air."

CHAPTER X
DO WE HAVE MARTINS HERE?

Popularity of the purple martin is rising so rapidly and public knowledge about this bird is still so slight that one of the most common questions today is, "Do we have martins in our area?"

Almost without exceptions, the answer to this question is "yes."

From such widely-scattered states as Montana, Pennsylvania, California, Washington, Maine, and Nebraska, the Griggsville Wild Bird Society receives dozens of inquiries of this nature. Why are so many people still uncertain about the presence of this bird, whose range is one of the widest of all native North American birds? Why has such a beneficial bird gone relatively unnoticed?

There are two principal reasons. The first is the bird's appearance. With no brilliant color to distinguish it from a distance, such as the colors of the cardinal, bluejay, oriole, or goldfinch, the bird is often confused by the untrained eye with other dark-colored birds like the blackbird, starling, tree swallow, kingbird, or swift. The other reason for a lack of widespread knowledge of the bird to match the widespread interest in it is that the martin is rarely noticed around the home and garden unless there is a martin house there.

The purple martin nests throughout the United States and southern Canada, with the exception of the dry areas of the Great Basin of the West. Bulletin 179 lists the northern limits of the nesting range as Edmonton and Camrose in central Alberta; Prince Albert and Quill Lake in central Saskatchewan; Lake St. Martin and Shoal Lake in southern Manitoba; Kenora, Sault Ste.

Marie, and Ottawa in southern Ontario; Montreal, Quebec, and Kamouraska in southern Quebec; Chatham in New Brunswick; and Prince Edward Island.

Throughout much of this range the presence of the martin is widely recognized. Martin houses are common sights throughout the south, midwest, Great Plains, and most of the eastern states. But some confusion exists in some areas, particularly the New England states and those on the Pacific coast, so we will discuss each of these areas in greater detail.

Despite the existence of robust colonies in Connecticut, Massachusetts, Maine, and on into Nova Scotia and New Brunswick, there still are many citizens of New England who are uncertain whether New England is within the natural range of the purple martin. It definitely is.

Martins at one time flourished in New England, but all of their major enemies have worked to diminish the population. Some severe springs, especially that of 1903, killed off great numbers of the birds. Rapid urbanization of New England eliminated many of their natural nesting sites. The introduction of both the English sparrow and the starling into this area first has given those birds a longer period of time in which to usurp whatever housing was available to the martins.

In fact, there are martin enthusiasts in New England who feel the sparrow and starling have been more important factors than either weather or urbanization in the martin's decline.

If the martin is to regain its former healthy numbers in the northeastern section of our nation, there is little doubt that it must have help from its human friends. Some citizens already are working in behalf of the bird, putting up modern housing that starlings will not inhabit, working to eliminate sparrows in a humane manner, and trying to salvage young grounded birds and older birds

164

suffering from starvation when unseasonably cold weather strikes.

Typical of these men is Jacob Bartovic of New Milford, Connecticut. He wrote, "We have a hard time with purple martins here in New Milford, but we are working hard to get as many as we can. And I am happy to say we are making headway. Ten years ago when I put up my martin house, we had 2 or 3 martin houses. Today we have two dozen with some 40-50 occupancies."

This is still a modest total for a community of much size, but as each year passes, a colony tends to mushroom rapidly if weather, pesticides, and natural enemies can be overcome as limiting factors.

Over the long haul the revitalization of the martin population in New England will require patience. Wayne Hanley of the Massachusetts Audubon Society does not believe the people of this fast-paced generation have the necessary patience and recently said so in an article in his widely published column: "It is conceivable that New England once again could be populated by purple martins. But it would require quite a string of martin houses—and more patience than our impatient era is likely to produce."

Mr. Hanley nevertheless recognized the opposing viewpoint within his own organization. James Baird of the Massachusetts Audubon Society believes that patient persons can profit from erecting a martin house, and he evidently believes there are enough patient people to get the job done. He has placed several large birdhouses in society sanctuaries, and some have been so successful that he encourages others to put up houses. Mr. Baird reports that it is unusual for the houses to be occupied the first summer, but that the young birds born each summer apparently spend their late summer days exploring and then the following years quite often fly back to new houses in the vicinity.

Lucien H. Thayer, writing in the Boston *Morning Globe,* said, "Here in New England we are on the fringe of the range because of the ocean barrier. But thousands of martins pass through here each year to Maine and Nova Scotia. And we have solid colonies at Plum Island and South Carver.

"Any person who is willing to gamble by raising a martin house has a good firm chance of success, providing the house is properly placed. An open field with a pond is ideal. There have been many good ones over cranberry bogs.

"Don't expect immediate results. I put one up in Rhode Island. The first year we had only visitors house hunting. The second year brought some nesting birds. Now we have a thriving colony."

Dr. Neville Kirsch of Hartford, Connecticut, has been promoting martins in his area for a number of years, both for their esthetic value and as an aid in mosquito control, and firmly believes that martins can be enticed back to Connecticut in large numbers if the citizens show sufficient interest.

Although the problem has not been so severe there, New York and parts of Pennsylvania also have shared the weather problems of New England. Some residents of these two states also share the New Englanders' uncertainty of the martins' range. Jack Reycraft wrote in 1966 in the Staten Island *Advance:*

"A Travis resident asks me why we don't do something to lure purple martins to Staten Island, because every day a purple martin consumes his own weight in insects. Well, as a matter of fact, we do have quite a colony of purple martins resident right now in Princes Bay, at the mouth of Lemon Creek.

"The Princes Bay martins live in apartment houses

erected by bird lovers. Dozens of martin couples will live in each house, each provided with its private quarters and entrance."

Incidentally, Mr. Reycraft is another of the growing number who can testify to the birds' effectiveness as insect-eaters. Mr. Reycraft said, "I can vouch, as a member of the former Princes Cabana Club, that there's not a mosquito in that area."

Mr. Reycraft feels that it is easier to attract martins to the shore area of Staten Island than it is inland and attributes this to lack of competition from sparrows along the shore. "Apparently house sparrows don't care for salt air," he says.

With enough proper housing and enough attention, man can help the birds overcome competition from sparrows and move inland in numbers as large as once existed there.

Leonard Hall, a naturalist whose home, "Possum Trot," is near Caledonia, Missouri, is familiar with natural conditions in various parts of the country. He states, "Perhaps instead of the constant spraying which many communities undertake to control insects, it would be wiser to attract the martins, which, contrary to some reports, are perfectly willing to nest in Westchester County, just outside of New York."

A letter from Charlotte Lord of Lincoln Center, Maine, illustrates the challenge to be met in bringing great numbers of martins back to New England. In 1966, she wrote to the Griggsville Wild Bird Society:

"A friend of mine, living about three miles from me, has four martin houses. Each year the houses have been full. Again this year the houses were filled and everything seemed normal.

"About the third week of May the people began to find the martins all around the yard. They would be

167

flying about as usual and all at once they would begin to fall to the ground.

"Upon examination the birds felt cold and of course were unable to fly. The people took the birds into the house and warmed pieces of cloth which were then placed around the birds to warm their bodies. This seemed to help them.

"In April we had very warm weather. Temperatures were much above normal, this being the reason, without a doubt, for the early flies, mosquitoes, etc. The birds came; shortly after we had cold, wet weather, and the insect population all but disappeared.

"Is there some way, should this happen again, we can help the martins?"

The answer is that martins have been successfully fed in such cases (see chapter XII), but there is not yet a sure-fire way to do it. A way must be found that will enable martin enthusiasts to save their birds during times of crisis. With the new interest in martins, it is certain to occur.

New techniques in feeding and caring for birds will be disseminated by the Griggsville Wild Bird Society as soon as new experiments are reported. We are confident that in a short time, possibly another season, this problem will be solved.

The results undoubtedly will be more marked in New England than anywhere else, but as 1966 proved, erratic weather can be a problem in every area of the nation.

The areas of southern Pennsylvania, Maryland, and Virginia do not share any of the doubt about the bird which seems to prevail in the remainder of the northeast. Thriving colonies are common in that area and, in fact, the one at Greencastle, Pennsylvania, is probably the oldest community-sponsored martin colony in the world, having been established in 1840.

Rear Admiral Neill Phillips, who is retired and now works with Mrs. Lyndon Johnson's beautification committee, wrote to the *Purple Martin Capital News,* "Our purple martins at our country place in Virginia mean a great deal to us, and their control of bug life is unbelievable."

Fortunately, all of the birds normally inhabiting an area are not necessarily subject to unfavorable weather such as struck the entire northern tier of states in 1966. Many of them remain in the southern areas, and some who do go north quickly return to the south ahead of the inclement weather. This was true in 1966, when martin enthusiasts throughout the south reported unusually large concentrations, even for an area in which they flourish in greater numbers than anywhere else.

The birds' normally large population in the south is due both to the existence of favorable weather and insect food supplies in many areas, and also to the fact that man has been catering to the martin longer in that area than anywhere else—a relationship that dates back to the Indians and extends through the plantation era right up to the present.

Although weather also takes a toll in the midwest and other northern states occasionally, the bird normally flourishes there, and his presence is well-known in most areas. More houses have been erected throughout this entire area in recent years, and its population is steadily growing despite unfavorable weather spells.

The purple martin also is popular in the Great Plains, although many people are becoming aware of its presence for the first time. The bird's existence is well-documented even in such states as Colorado, Wyoming, and Montana, normally considered dry areas. Little has been done to encourage martins in those areas, however, and more will be necessary before they exist in large numbers.

In 1966, the Jaycees of Saratoga, Wyoming, a resort area in the southern part of the state, purchased 14 martin houses and erected them in their city. They failed to attract any birds the first season.

Lynn Brown, a member of the Wyoming Department of Conservation and a director of the Saratoga Jaycees, is optimistic, however. He informs us that the group was advised by the University of Wyoming that there have been numerous martin sightings in Wyoming, and that they still feel chances for success of their project are good.

While Saratoga had no martins the first season, the town did have many tree swallows nesting in the boxes, and these, of course, were welcomed.

Another member of their conservation department is familiar with Edmonton, Alberta, at the northern limit of the martins' range. He says that the martin population gradually declined in that area, despite the existence of the many lakes in central Alberta and otherwise highly-favorable conditions. Then, three years ago the trend was reversed and in just two years, residents had very little trouble attracting martins to any house erected.

J. C. Finlay of Edmonton has 18 compartments, with 17 of them filled in 1966. Each of his compartments is equipped with a photoelectric cell which records the arrival and departure of birds in the cavity and thus accurately records levels of activity. He also has a weather station that measures continuous light, temperature, barometric pressure, and amounts of rainfall.

He accumulated data from eight compartments in 1965 and 17 in 1966 and will soon publish a report of his findings on the correlation of the martins' activities with the other climatic factors mentioned.

Incidentally, the last martins left Edmonton on August

27, 1966, about a week later than normal, according to Mr. Finlay, and approximately the same time that the last martins left west-central Illinois.

There are well-documented cases of martin sightings in all states west of the Rockies, including Montana, and along the Pacific coastal areas. When the bird must depend upon natural nesting sites, it will nest first along rivers, lakes, and other bodies of water, but proper efforts on the part of man can encourage its development almost anywhere away from these rivers, except in extremely dry areas. It appears that wherever there are enough insects to constitute a nuisance to man, the purple martin can find enough food to survive.

The western martin, slightly smaller than the purple martin, but so much the same bird that it has the same generic name, *progne subis,* inhabits the Pacific coastal areas of Baja California, California, Oregon, Washington, and British Columbia.

It is not nearly so well-known as its cousin the purple martin, but it too is beginning to come into the public spotlight. The reason for its obscurity is that it still nests in natural sites in most of the area.

Only in Oregon have significant and successful attempts been made to get the bird to colonize near man's homes.

Let's examine this bird, which has as much potential for the west as the purple martin has exhibited for the remainder of the nation.

Dr. John Hardy, ornithologist at Occidental College in Los Angeles, reports that "western martins in California inhabit only the mountainous areas because lack of trees in the low-lying coastal areas provided no housing sites for them in the days before man settled. The birds will colonize when given the opportunity and there are records of two martin colonies nesting in Los Angeles. However, this is extremely rare." (The opportunity to colonize is

171

rare because natural multiple dwelling sites don't usually exist, and people haven't yet put up many houses in that area.)

"Western martins also will build in woodpeckers' cavities in the Saguaro cactus in southern Arizona. Some man-made houses are in use there.

"Western martins do use martin houses in the Pacific northwest because over the years they have been able to make the transition from the plentiful big trees in that part of the country to houses that man erected for them."

The Distribution of Birds in California, prepared in 1944 by the Cooper Ornithological Club of Berkeley, said of the "northern purple martin," that it is "ordinarily considered fairly common, but many seemingly-suitable localities lack this swallow; 'colonies' or established pairs are widely scattered. There is some indication of spreading to occupy certain districts built up by people in recent years. Probably the aggregate number of purple martins is increasing."

The Cooper publication also said, "While showing colonial tendencies, by resorting to a given neighborhood affording sufficient nesting sites in numbers up to 20 pairs, this seldom occurs; often only one pair is found in a locality." Apparently the writer is still talking about the bird's natural habitat in that statement, but he continues, "A departure on a par with that shown by some other swallows is the adoption of human-provided nesting niches, incidentally, in the eaves and cornices of buildings or, so far rarely, purposely supplied 'martin houses.' This adoption has brought the birds into localities, such as certain lowland cities, where they were not known to breed before."

While both Dr. Hardy and the Cooper Ornithological Club seem to agree that the erection of man-made housing is rare, they both observe that this is successful in areas

172

This young bird landed to rest on the lawn of the Trio testing grounds during its first training flight in July of 1966, and Wayne Bradshaw picked it up. The bird seemed almost totally unafraid and posed for a variety of photographs before flying on.

where it has been tried and where the birds have not been known to breed before. Consequently, their findings provide an optimistic note for both man and martin on the west coast.

The martin arrives in California in late March or early April and remains until September. It arrives somewhat later, of course, in the northwest—usually in the latter part of April—and departs slightly earlier—usually in late August.

The western martin has been reported nesting as far north as Victoria and Nanaimo in British Columbia and as far south as Baja California. Its wintering range is not definitely known.

The primitive habitat of the western martin includes a variety of oak, pine, sycamore, and other trees commonly

173

used by woodpeckers. Heavy forests are not normally inhabited because martins need flying room around their nests, and because they are somewhat safer from predators in more lightly-forested areas.

Holes made by woodpeckers are most commonly used as nesting sites. These usually occur singly, and this explains the absence of martin colonies in the wild.

However, as noted above, the western martin will colonize in man-made houses and is doing so in increasing numbers. The west coast appears to be an area in which a rapid increase in the martin population can be achieved with a reasonable amount of effort. Provision of adequate housing and dissemination of basic facts on their proper location and on the care of martins can perhaps mean the rise of the martin to the level of importance and popularity it has achieved in the rest of the country.

CHAPTER XI
THE IDEAL MARTIN HOUSE INSTALLATION

EVOLUTION OF HOUSING

Just as human housing has evolved from caves, tepees, thatched houses, and log huts through a variety of materials and designs to modern structures of brick, glass, concrete, steel, and aluminum, so have livestock production facilities evolved. Modern swine farrowing houses, milking parlors, and "chicken factories" are a far cry from the barns of yesteryear. They fulfilled a variety of needs quite adequately for the farming situations that prevailed in those days but are inefficient for today's requirements. Modern farming operations could not obtain maximum profits and optimum production without the flexibility and functionalism of modern buildings and equipment.

More recently, this trend toward functionalism also has begun to emerge in man's efforts to propagate certain species of the wild bird.

The earliest known martin housing provided by man consisted of hollowed gourds suspended near Indian tepees. In the spring of 1966, Dr. William Beecher, in commenting upon the arrival of the martins, pointed out that many of the birds then arriving in Chicago were direct descendants of birds first attracted there by the Indians.

"This was mostly swamp at that time," he said. "The insects must have been so thick that about all the Indians could do at night was sit in smoky tepees with their bodies smeared with bear grease.

"Then the Indians got smart and started stringing gourds with holes in them on poles so the martins would be attracted to the area to eat a lot of the insects.

"Thanks to the Indians, the martins have been coming here by instinct ever since," Dr. Beecher concluded.

Gourds are still used today; they are very common in the south.

The greatest disadvantage of gourds is the loss of young birds from this type of a nesting cavity. Being porous, these cavities are perfect for harboring parasites. They are not easy to clean, as each must be taken down individually and old materials removed through the entrance hole. Consequently, nesting materials often build up over the years and further increase attractiveness to parasites.

On hot summer days gourds also have a tendency to become too hot for the young birds. Both heat and parasites can force young birds to seek relief outside, where no protective devices prevent them from falling to the ground.

Mrs. Lorene Pendergraft of Chapel Hill, North Carolina, has a very nice colony of martins which each year inhabits 30 to 40 gourds suspended beside a pond at her home. Recently, a visiting member of the society spotted a young martin on the ground under one of the gourds and rescued it. Mrs. Pendergraft remarked, "That happens all the time."

This is a common complaint from the numerous areas of the country where gourds are used.

Wooden houses, widely used since colonists first arrived in this part of the world, also possess some of the gourd's disadvantages. There are many elaborate, beautiful, and well-maintained wooden houses in use in this country, housing healthy martin colonies.

But in many cases, the weight of a wooden house makes it difficult to erect and to raise and lower for maintenance. This tends to discourage the performance of proper annual maintenance. These houses slowly fall into disrepair, and their consequent shoddy appearance soon makes them

176

A sparrow trap can be mounted directly on the pole supporting a martin house and will enable the martin enthusiast to transport sparrows away from the vicinity of the martin colony. Fresh bread is all the bait that is needed. (Note the tent mounted atop the van in background of photo at right. This is used as a blind and is one of the devices which Trio personnel use to photograph birds at very close range.

more attractive to starlings than to martins. The porosity of wood, in addition, encourages parasites, and colonies inhabiting these houses suffer from their effects, especially the loss of young birds.

Moreover, most wooden houses are not equipped with guard rails, thus increasing the chances of young birds falling to the ground prematurely. Few young birds are reported on the ground under aluminum houses—which are the only common type equipped with rails—and this has proved to be one of the greatest advantages of modern martin housing.

In Griggsville, we have found the time young birds spend in the nest between hatching and flight varies from 28 to 32 days. The majority of data in other bird books, however, lists this period as 24 to 28 days, a variance of four days from our findings. This difference may very well be attributed to the almost exclusive use of aluminum housing in Griggsville. Both the coolness of the aluminum house and the presence of guard rails work to keep the young birds in the nest until they are ready to fly away safely.

Many owners of more traditional types of housing often report even unfeathered birds on the ground. This never happens in Griggsville. The presence of any young martin on the ground is unusual, and if it does happen, the birds invariably are fully-feathered and capable of a considerable degree of flight. Losses of young birds are nil.

Indians using gourds as bird houses did not need to be concerned about the advantages that might accrue to the birds. Martins abounded in the land at that time, and the survival rate of young birds was unimportant.

Early settlers, to almost the same extent, did not need to be concerned about the welfare of the bird population as a whole.

More people are now considering two factors instead of one in the selection of housing. They want to attract the birds, but they also are concerned about replacing the birds' natural habitat, which has been largely destroyed and with rebuilding the birds' population. Housing factors that satisfy these considerations are gaining in popularity, and this is part of the reason for the martin house owners' growing insistence on such features as cool, light, maintenance-free aluminum; guard rails; good ventilation; and easy cleanout features.

The installation of an ideal modern martin house alone does not always mean that martins will appear. To be sure, the typical martin probably does not care how difficult a house is for its owner to raise and lower, nor does it correctly anticipate how parasite-free a house will be in June nor how cool it will be in July. Neither

In times of necessity, martins will nest in a variety of places. In 1966 this one chose a traffic light in Houston, and the city obligingly turned the light off and put up a substitute light until the nesting season was over. (Photo by Houston Chronicle)

does the martin care how ornate his house is by human standards.

However, a great number of factors do influence a martin's choice of nesting sites, and persons who have been unsuccessful in attracting martins or who plan to make their first try at it should study thoroughly the factors influencing the martins' choices before exerting any more effort.

In order, we shall deal with factors determining the ideal house, its location, and other neighborhood features that may influence nesting.

THE IDEAL HOUSE

Ornithologists and naturalists who have established specifications for a well-designed martin house obtained their data from an authoritative source—the martins themselves. Seeking out natural nesting sites, these scientists made careful measurements, observed closely the home life of the martins and, after years of patient research, decided upon 6″ x 6″ x 6″ as the best nesting compartment size. A compartment should not vary from these dimensions too much.

The best size for the opening is a hole 2⅛″ in diameter. Noting that the lower edges of holes in frequently-used, natural nesting cavities often became worn off by use and that easier access was thus provided to the compartment, Trio patterned its keyhole entrance after this natural characteristic.

Good ventilation and drainage also are requisites for the colony's health, particularly for the fledglings. While martins probably do not survey a home and say, "No, this has inadequate drainage and ventilation and will not do," they do abandon nesting sites in which there occurs a heavy loss of their young, whether the loss is caused by predators, drowning in the nests, pesticides, or any other

Porch railings and the coolness and comfort of modern houses keep the young in the houses a few days longer, resulting in fewer fatalities among young birds.

cause. Proper housing can greatly reduce the chances of such calamities.

As a general rule, we have found that the more compartments offered, the better the chances of attracting a colony.

We determined that six compartments are the fewest that can be erected with any reasonable expectation of occupancy and that chances increase as the number of compartments increases. Our files contain a number of reports from persons who obtained no martins after erecting a single house, but who, after erecting a second house, filled it and sometimes the original house as well. Not enough cases have been reported that we can definitely attribute this phenomenon to the addition of more compartments and not to other changing factors in the neighborhood, but present evidence weighs convincingly in favor of the second house.

A possible explanation is that these martin house owners attracted colonies that wished to remain intact but could not find adequate housing until the second houses were erected.

181

Martins seem to care little which direction the openings face. No pattern of preference has been noted in Griggsville.

When necessary, martins will nest in a variety of situations. Possibly the abnormally large martin population in the south in 1966 accounted for the presence of nesting pairs in traffic signals in Vicksburg, Mississippi, and Houston, Texas (both pairs nested in front of green lights).

In Houston, a busy service station had a thriving colony of martins nesting in the steel beams of its modernistic shelter over the drive. Martins, far from being repelled by human activity, seem to be attracted by it.

The highest nesting site we have heard about is reported in Bulletin 179. Martins nested at 130 feet above the ground in Seattle, Washington. The bulletin quotes S. F. Rathbun: "A rather high brick building in the lower business district was surmounted by a tall flagpole capped with a ball. This ball was at a height of about 130 feet above the street. One day when I was watching martins glide above the building one of them flew directly to the ball and disappeared. By the use of a pair of field glasses a check or crack could be seen in the side of the ball, which accounted for the bird's disappearance; it was using the ball as a nesting place. Use of it continued for a number of years, until the ball was replaced by another."

The lowest nesting site to come to our attention was reported this year, by H. J. Weyenberg of Mequon, Wisconsin. "In West Palm Beach," he said, "I actually saw a pair of martins in a martin house on the pier very low down and near a bench! Some sea captain said they come every year."

A pair of martins in Charlotte, North Carolina, may not have set a record for nesting at the highest or lowest elevations, but they undoubtedly set a record for nesting at *more* elevations than any other pair in a single season. This pair as reported by J. A. C. Dunn in the Charlotte *Observer,* nested near the business end of the 90-ft. boom of a construction crane!

The construction crew could not let up its operations to accommodate the birds, when they started to nest, but the birds wouldn't let up either.

"I saw them chasing the crane when it swung, carrying a piece of straw, trying to catch up with it," said Crosby Dunn, one of the equipment operators of the Charlotte Water Department pump station near Highway 16, where the construction was under way. The workmen watched the development of the family with interest. Superintendent Ernest Godwin named the female "Bossy" because her activities around the nest made her look as though she were directing the crane operator where to move the crane.

Baxter B. Wilson Jr. of Charlotte, North Carolina, has kept some of the most extensive martin records in America for the past 10 years. He uses both gourds and a wooden house, and next year plans to add an aluminum house to these martin accommodations.

Semi-hardened waste materials are carried away from the nest by adult birds, and deposited far from the nest, a protective measure practiced by some species of birds to prevent detection of their nests by their enemies.

The martins hatched two eggs and immediately began carrying insects to their offspring—when they could catch up with them. Workmen believe that one of the young fell out of the nest soon after it was hatched but that the other survived.

"At least she ain't got no cat problem," said one of the workmen.

THE IDEAL LOCATION

One of the most important considerations in attracting martins is the location of the house. Martins are free-wheeling flyers, usually on the move. The Indians called them "the birds that never rest." When they are not darting and swooping after insects, they are soaring about their houses. They love to ride the wind and often will remain almost stationary in the air, buoyed up by the air currents.

Birds of this type need plenty of air space around their homes. Ideally, the house should be installed in the center of an open area at least 25 feet diameter, with no obstructions to their free flight. This free area should, of course extend skyward with little or no tree foliage above.

Utility wires are not objectionable; they do not interfere with the birds' flight, and the birds love to perch on wires.

Spacious areas are not only preferable for flight pur-

184

Martins soaring in the sky above the Maryland countryside are part of the colony of Elvin J. Stottlemyer of Middletown, Maryland. When not feeding, martins often soar in the wind, apparently just for the pleasure of it.

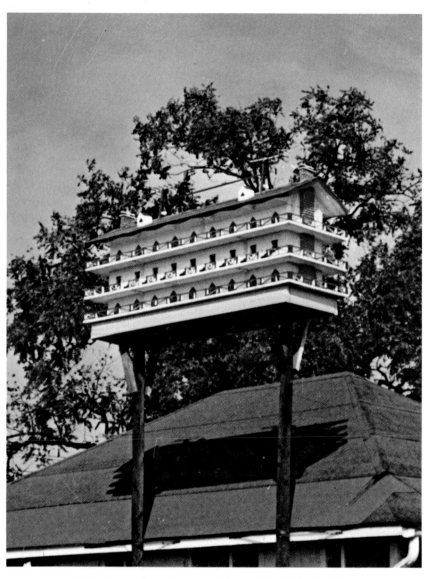

This house, located near Gibson City, Illinois, illustrates the beauty and grandeur achieved by some hobbyists. It required a wrecker and four men to lift and fix in position and any cleanout of nests which is required is an extensive operation.

186

Art Schreyer, whose hometown of Des Plaines is a suburb of Chicago, nicknamed this house "Martina Tower," after the Windy City's famed Marina Towers. Note that the five martins on left in this photo seem to illustrate a photographic time sequence of a martin landing on the lower porch. (Photo by Art Schreyer)

Gourds, used as martin compartments since Indian days, still are used in a variety of ways.

"*Handsome,*" *the purple martin which was struck by a car in the Purple Martin Capital in 1965, was nursed back to flying condition by Craig Windmiller (above) and other members of the high school biology class. Bird with bandaged wing is shown below. Although martins are slow to get off the ground, they seldom land on the ground and consequently cars are not normally a menace to these birds.*

William T. Young of Madison, Nebraska, was given a boost by this little martin during a recent convalescence. Mr. Young was sitting under a shade tree in his yard during the summer of 1966 when this little fellow flew from a tree limb and landed on his shoulder. Mr. Young then walked into the house and his daughter snapped this photo.

189

The martin house testing grounds in front of the Trio plant are located just south of Griggsville on route 107.

The welcome mat is always out for visitors to the Purple Martin Capital. A new tourist center where visitors can relax in modern comfort, see the movie of the purple martin story, and acquire information about martins and other birds, is now open near the business district in Griggsville.

Martins at the fairgrounds in Griggsville are undisturbed by the activities of the fair, and usually are feeding young birds during that time—the first week in July. The martins stay up later than usual during show nights, soaring silently above the race track and stage, or just sitting on the boxes and utility wires, watching the crowd.

poses; they also provide more protection from predators like snakes, cats, and raccoons, which can more easily reach the houses from overhanging limbs and roofs of buildings.

A pond or other body of water in the immediate vicinity will make the house more attractive to martins, as they drink and bathe on the fly, swooping low over the water's surface and scooping up a few drops on each pass. Lawn sprinklers also are irresistible to some martin colonies. They will swoop through the spray, which seems to be as satisfactory as a pond or any other water. Although there are reliable reports of martins using bird baths, they are rare. Bird baths normally play no role in

T. E. inspects a box on one of his bluebird trails in Adams County, Illinois.

A Salute to T.E. . . .

Our good friend, Dr. T. E. Musselman of Quincy, Illinois, truly possesses one of America's outstanding records of service to conservation. To give an idea of his career, here are just a few of his accomplishments since entering the University of Illinois in 1906:

While still a student he was one of three founders of the national education honorary, Kappa Delta Pi, and was its first president. His degrees include bachelor of arts in English and biology, U. of I.; master of accounts, Gem City Business College, Quincy; master of arts, U. of I.; and doctor of science, Carthage College. He has served as president of Gem City Business College.

T.E., a well known writer and lecturer for many years, has been a director of Inland Bird Banding Association and Illinois Audubon Society and a member of Illinois Academy of Science and American Ornithologists Union. He has erected more than 1000 bluebird boxes in Illinois and Missouri and many prothonotary warbler boxes in the Mississippi swamplands and still maintains these boxes.

Dr. Musselman received the Hornaday Award for Conservation in 1955; the Silver Beaver award in 1958; and was named "Ornithologist of the Year for Work in Ornithology and Conservation" by Illinois Bird Banding Association and Iowa Audubon Societies in 1965. He is included in Who's Who in America.

Dr. Musselman has been featured in both Ford Times and Readers Digest. He has written a nature diary for 50 years and the Illinois Natural History Survey has requested the diary be left in its possession for posterity.

Dr. Musselman has done much not only for purple martins, but for all of the birds of America, and we salute one of the nation's foremost naturalists, still active at 79, and still adding to the story of a great conservationist.

attracting martins to a yard.

Neither will putting out bird feed. As mentioned earlier, martins normally live only on flying insects.

Sprinkling bits of egg shell in the yard will help, however. This is a convenient and economical way to provide the minerals that martins cannot get in their regular diet of insects.

Another tip that will help attract martins: Place a small deposit of twigs, straw, short pieces of string, and similar materials in the yard before their nest building time. They will use this material in their nests.

A little mud puddle prepared in a secluded area of the lawn or garden will provide the martins with the "mortar" they need to build their nests. Incidentally, bird watchers will seldom see a purple martin on the ground except during their nest-building days when they seek grasses and dabs of mud.

MAKE A THOROUGH STUDY

No one can yet predict with 100 percent reliability whether a particular housing situation will appeal to martins or put up a house that is guaranteed to attract them. There are too many factors that influence nesting choices.

Many persons who have been unsuccessful in attracting martins can greatly improve their chances by using a thorough, scientific approach. Make a comprehensive list of factors in your neighborhood that may influence the birds.

The presence of dogs and cats usually does not discourage a colony unless, of course, a cat can get to the nest. One trip by a cat up a wooden pole to visit a martin house and that house probably will have no more martins for a long time. The same applies to raccoons, snakes, and owls (owls don't often raid martin houses, preferring to prey on rodents—they are among our most beneficial birds in this respect).

A metal guard around a wooden pole, high enough to prevent a cat from jumping above it, will keep away most predators.

What about smoke or unusual smells in your neighborhood? There are a number of cases on record in which the presence of smoke made a martin house untenantable. These are fresh air birds. Fresh paint on a birdhouse has been known to drive birds away. Apparently, the fumes were objectionable.

There is no hard and fast rule concerning the effects of noise on martins. In some cases, construction work, in the immediate vicinity has driven martins from their homes. In others, the martins seemed to thrive on the excitement and activity. Among the heavily-occupied houses in Griggsville are those at the fairgrounds race track. The birds seem to enjoy the excitement of harness racing. At the Indianapolis Speedway, during the Memorial Day classic of 1966, a female martin fed her young on the lower level of the photographer's stand throughout the entire race and didn't seem at all concerned, according to columnist Bob Corya of the Indianapolis *News*.

The martins that nested in the swinging boom of a

Chances of attracting martins increase with the number of nesting compartments offered. Two-hole houses such as this were tested in Griggsville and attracted no birds at all.

crane in Charlotte, North Carolina, probably don't think too much of construction work, but it wasn't the noise that bothered them.

Another neighborhood menace that can discourage martins is the presence of children equipped with BB guns and an unawareness of the value of birds. If this is a problem, a few words of explanation to the children concerned will usually win them over to the side of the birds. They are not ordinarily as thoughtless as some persons think; they just share the unawareness of the many adults who haven't given any thought to the benefits of our birds.

A prospective martin host should analyze each aspect of the location of his house. Perhaps some very simple factor is preventing him from enjoying the birds. In our trips across the country, we've noticed many perfectly suitable houses virtually touching the leaves of trees. In most cases, these are at the edge of an open space and could be moved as little as 10 feet to make the house many, many times more attractive to the birds.

We do not pretend to offer a comprehensive list of possible nesting influences here. Some factors, of course, are still unknown, which accounts for the fact that the success of a house cannot be predicted with 100 percent accuracy.

We do hope to encourage martin enthusiasts to develop the habit of checking for all possible factors and increasing their knowledge and thus their chances of attracting birds. In most cases, a few simple steps can greatly increase these chances.

When one does attract martins, he will find that they are well worth whatever time and money he put into the effort. Houses valued as high as $500—one fashioned after a church and erected in Lehigh Acres, Florida, is insured for that amount—are in use. Houses valued at

$100 or more are increasingly common. If some of the beautiful and elaborate houses built by hobbyists were appraised according to the amount of time and skilled labor put into their construction, their values would run as high as $1,000.

Weather and other factors being normal, chances of getting martins the first season after erecting a house are good. Often two or three years are required, however, before the martins decide on a house.

Once a house has attracted martins, they will return to it year after year. Many of their young also will return, although some well-documented cases report that the majority of young birds seek other housing on their return.

Baxter B. Wilson Jr. of Charlotte, North Carolina, who has had William Anderson of Charlotte, a registered bander, to band the birds in his big colony, has kept extensive records over a 10-year period. He has 23 banded birds in his colony. As they have been able to band only the young birds each year, they were able to determine that all of these 23 birds were raised there and returned to become part of the permanent colony. One martin has occupied the same compartment for the past seven years.

Since Mr. Wilson's colony is filled each year, there is a good possibility that the rest of the young birds banded each year move on to other colonies because there is no room in their original colony. This overflow helps to populate new colonies and increases the overall population of the purple martin. (Mr. Wilson has noted that the youngest birds are always the last to arrive. It is still a mystery how they find their way back by themselves.)

The homing instinct in the martin is strong. There are reports of flocks returning the following spring to the site of their previous home and flying around its exact spot even though the house and pole are no longer there.

CHAPTER XII
PEOPLE AND MARTINS

Man and martin have co-existed with mutual regard for many years. This cordial relationship has warmed through the years until today it is not at all unusual for a man to spend $100 or more to provide ultra-deluxe housing for families of martins.

This symbiosis has provided us with numerous stories, many of which are concerned with man's efforts—sometimes successful, sometimes not—to raise baby martins that have fallen from their nests to the ground.

MARTHA FINDS A NEW HOME

In Salamanca, New York, the John F. Vosburg family has for a number of years provided summer homes for their martin friends. From time to time, a fledgling would fall from its nest to the ground, and the Vosburgs would make every effort to save it. Despite the solicitous and patient attention paid the birds by these good folk, the fledglings invariably expired in a few days. Some essential element in their natural, lifegiving diet was apparently missing from the food being hand-fed them.

Then one summer day, they found a female baby martin on the ground and—but let's allow Ruth Vosburg to tell the story:

". . . we named her Martha. She was probably two weeks old and was partially feathered. We decided to duplicate the previous year's experiment of catching grasshoppers to feed her, the only addition being that each day we gave her some fine canary gravel. Much to our surprise, that was all that was needed. For the next several weeks, our family, consisting of four, spent a large part of our spare time scouring the fields for grasshoppers. We were concerned that people seeing us would think that we were somewhat 'touched' and did not lose an opportunity to explain what we were doing and why. We really don't know if the explanation did more harm than good!

"I might note now that before arriving at grasshoppers as being the proper food for baby martins, we first tried dog food, cat food, turtle food, hamburger, baby chick feed, etc., to no avail. Thus grasshoppers.

"For the first three weeks of Martha's sojourn with us, she ate close to 100 grasshoppers a day. Gravel was fed to her by dipping grasshoppers in moistened canary gravel. As Martha became more mature, this number decreased by half, for which we were most thankful. By this time it began to seem more natural for us to go around on all fours than, as my husband said, to walk on our hind legs!

"Since my husband insisted that, to make the grasshoppers more palatable and easier to eat, the hind legs should be pulled off before offering up a meal to Martha, I soon became heartily tired of grasshoppers. I resolved to studiously avoid seeing any more baby martins on the ground.

"However, now that Martha has left us, and in view of the wonderful experiences in raising her, we realize that we will be very apt to repeat our actions should the opportunity present itself again.

"When we got Martha, we had to force-feed her the first couple of times. We simply pried her beak open with a tooth pick and dropped a small grasshopper into her mouth. It was not very long until she would open her mouth and peep at us whenever we came near. Then it would require 10-15 grasshoppers to satisfy her truly prodigious appetite. When she became strong enough, we would lay newspapers on the kitchen table and make her come at first a few inches and then clear across the table for her food. This we felt was very necessary to instill in her the habit of coming to us, rather than we to her, because we could foresee that, in the not too distant future, she would be flying and obviously landing in spots where we could not reach her. It was probably three or four weeks before she became strong enough to fly, which ability she demonstrated by flying at first a few inches from the table to us. This distance we increased when we felt she was capable of flying farther.

"In the meantime, she had demonstrated several lovable traits, among which was her ability to soak up petting like a sponge. She would cuddle down in my hand with every possible inch of her pressed tightly to it, while I stroked her head and back lightly with my fingers. In fact, I spent many hours reading in the evening, with a book in one hand and Martha in the other. This trait, incidentally, she never lost as she matured.

"A game which my husband and I often played with her involved one of us sitting at each end of the kitchen table with Martha between us. We would take turns putting our hand on the table, palm down with finger tips and wrist almost touching, making an arch of the hand and thus an opening which Martha would spot and hurry (with a funny duck-like waddle) to get into. Once under our hand, she would sort of shimmy herself into a really cuddly position, then peer out as if to say 'There. I'm all comfortable and warm and nothing can hurt me here.'

"When Martha became strong enough, we took her outdoors (when she was hungry) and had her fly from one to the other to be fed. Our concern at this time was to have her develop the habit of flying to us for food, because as mentioned previously, we were afraid that she might fly away someplace where we couldn't see her or reach her and starve. During this period, I would often times walk around our garden with Martha on my hand by way of giving her all the fresh air and sunshine that I could. Much to my horror and amazement, one day she suddenly 'took off' and disappeared around the hedges and trees so quickly that I didn't have the least idea where she had gone. Up until then she had taken flights of only five or ten feet, all of which were simply babyish flutterings from one to another of us for food. This flight, however, was the real thing. It was the darting, effortless flight of an adult martin. You can imagine how I felt. I was thrilled that she could fly so well, however frightened that she might have landed on the ground someplace where I couldn't find her, which would mean her eventual destruction by a dog or cat. I hunted as long as I could to no avail.

"Finally I had to stop the search to prepare luncheon for my family. When my husband came home, he started hunting and finally spotted her perched on a neighbor's roof against their chimney. After about 15 minutes of calling, Martha gathered together enough courage to fly from the chimney to my husband's shoulder—a distance of probably 200 feet. What a relief!

"After that she learned very rapidly, and it was not long until I would put her out the kitchen window and she would fly onto our garage roof. On the peak of the garage, we have a weather vane with figure of a horse mounted over an indication arrow. This horse eventually proved to be Martha's favorite perch, and we got many a chuckle about Martha and her horse, ofttimes watching her as the wind swung her and her steed about.

"As time went on, she would spend more hours outside, flying about some, and if we did not go out to feed her, she would land on the kitchen window sill, emitting peeping sounds by way of demanding entrance and over-due meal. Of course, she was very happy to come into

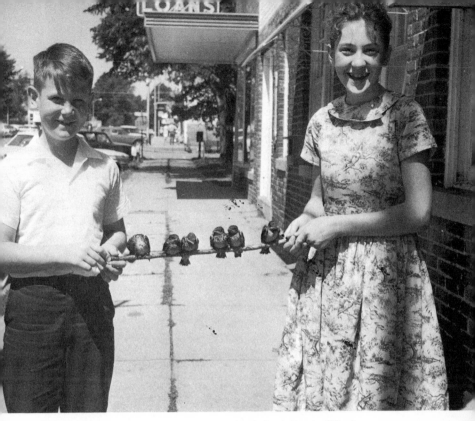

The children of Mr. and Mrs. C. I. Bethel of Pearl, Illinois, raised these six martins in 1964. They were never able to determine whether the birds returned to Pearl the following year. (Photo by Pike County Republican)

the house in late afternoon or early evening to stay for the night.

"When grasshoppers became scarce in nearby fields, we went out in the country and found them plentiful in pasture land near a camp owned by my family. We, of course, took Martha with us on these expeditions, during which time she would have really long flights, soaring over the fields and watching us humans work for her dinner, occasionally landing on one of our shoulders and demanding a sample of those truly luscious grasshoppers.

There were a few times that we were afraid that she was lost or simply gone, however after we had called her, she would come flying from some not-too-distant tree and serenely land on our shoulder or head as if to say 'Don't worry about me—I know just what I'm doing.'

"I might say here that it was the strangest sensation to have a fully-mature bird come to me on call. It finally developed that when we were out in the garden doing anything from working to playing croquet, that Martha would land on our head or shoulder, unannounced and of course ready to eat, although I must confess many times it was purely for the sake of sociability.

"A couple of incidents in the garden which I shall always cherish in memory are—one day I happened to stroll out between household chores and naturally looked about to see where Martha might be. I couldn't see her on any of the rooftops nearby and happened to look up and spotted what I was sure to be a purple martin far, far overhead, in fact so far that it was very slightly larger than a speck. I held out my hand and called to her, and much to my amazement this speck in the sky started to fall rapidly towards me. It was only a second or so before it resolved itself into a plummeting purple martin, which of course turned out to be Martha diving down to land on my outstretched hand. What a tremendous thrill that was.

"Another time when walking down our garden path, I heard a robin cry off to my right and looked up in time to see Martha flying down the side of our garden with a mother robin in hot pursuit. Just about the time they reached the end of our garden, Martha spotted me and immediately reversed the direction of her flight, much to the amazement of the robin, and came scooting back to land on my shoulder.

"One of the most interesting parts of Martha's stay

with us was in the fall when we became concerned that she might decide to spend the winter with us. As mentioned previously, grasshoppers were the only things she would eat (although of course their natural food is small insects caught in flight) and they must be alive. You can appreciate our concern, knowing that she would starve when the grasshoppers were gone. Everyday Martha would join the adult martins flying about; however, she would come back to us very often for food and petting. We, of course, kept hoping that she would stay with them and finally migrate.

"Labor Day arrived with only a dozen or so adult martins in the neighborhood. As a general rule the martins would never stay after the frosts; in fact, long before the first frost they would be gone. Much to our amazement, at least a dozen adult birds stayed in the vicinity after we had had quite a few frosts. Each day they would fly by, calling to Martha. She would fly away with them and be gone several hours, coming back and flying down to us to be fed and housed overnight.

"Finally, the night arrived when Martha did not return, at which time of course we were sure that finally she was strong enough to make the long flight south and had really gone out of our lives. We were most amazed the next morning when she landed on our windowsill, demanding the supper and breakfast which she had been deprived of by what must have been an unusually long flight. After several more days of flights, with the adults who were obviously only staying to wait for Martha to become strong enough to accompany them, she finally did not return, after which time, of course, we no longer saw any of the martins that fall. This was a tremendous experience and one which we will never forget.

"We had, except for a few details, almost identically

203

the same experience in raising a Bohemian waxwing a few years ago. This bird was very much easier to raise because it would eat berries which need not be fresh. In times of stress we even fed it canned blueberries, raspberries, etc.

"As spring nears, we are again anxiously awaiting the arrival of our purple martins and the hours of pleasure we derive from watching them."

As related in this story, the Vosburgs' young martin once dived from a great height to land in one of their hands, but martin enthusiasts sometimes report martins diving in this manner, not to land, but to pass within a few feet in an apparent scare tactic.

John W. Allen, Southern Illinois University's noted historian and a martin enthusiast, recently commented on this trait:

"Occasional parent birds may 'dive bomb' an animal or person passing near their home. Such birds are nothing more than a bundle of harmless fury coming about a mile a minute. There is no record of one ever making contact. The threatening overtone of their twitter as they zoom at you gives you plenty of time to duck. Having passed you, their threatening overtone seems almost to change to one of elation. Could it be they have a sense of humor and like to see men and dogs cower?"

F. L. Fowler of Houston is now 71 and has spent most of his years as a bird enthusiast. He remembers many unusual episodes involving birds, but one of those he considers most remarkable was an act of feathered cooperation that he witnessed in 1964.

Marshall Verniaud of the Houston *Post* wrote:

"A violent storm toppled the one pole of bird houses he had at that time. Newly-hatched fledglings of the purple martin families were scattered in wet grass. Fowler protected them from a cat but knew that the odds against

204

their survival were great.

"Almost immediately, more than 100 martins came from everywhere to help the storm-stricken birds save their fledglings.

" 'Some of them got after the cat and chased him so far that he never came back,' Fowler said. 'Others found bugs to feed the little birds. It was a regular community rescue operation.'

"The next day, after the storm subsided, Fowler collected as many of the fledglings as he could find and put them in the repaired birdhouses, two in each 'apartment.'

" 'I don't know where they belonged,' he said. 'The parent martins took care of them until they could fly away.

" 'As soon as the little birds were safe again, the crowd of martins disappeared. The rescue job was finished'."

Fowler's experience was doubly unusual in that martins usually do not feed young martins on the ground. In fact, their apparent unwillingness to feed grounded birds has led to many interesting stories involving humans and martins. Typical of these is the experience of Mrs. Lawrence Zeleny of Hyattsville, Maryland, in which a baby cardinal got into the act before it was over.

In Mrs. Zeleny's words:

"My husband and I have successfully raised baby robins and bluejays to maturity. Until this summer, (1966) we have never had the pleasure of bringing up baby martins. Purple martins?? What a challenge! Two babies, feathered but not yet ready to fly, dropped out of the house after a week of intense heat. I believe they emerged in an attempt to cool off, only to fall from the little porch.

"The first day, it was necessary to force feed them, prying open the tiny clamped bills and pushing the morsels of food down the reluctant gullets, while they

205

fixed me with a malevolent eye. I used a mixture of ground steak, an amount the size of a golf ball into which I added a quarter teaspoon of di-calcium phosphate containing vitamin D, a small puppy biscuit shaved fine, and a pinch of Pervinal, a vitamin-mineral mixture designed for puppies. With this mixture, given every 40 minutes or so, I added one meal of hard-boiled egg yolk and one morsel of cooked liver. Each bit was dipped in water to ease the journey down the throat.

"The second morning, I was awakened by hungry protests. Both mouths were open. My gray hair must have sprouted purple feathers, for I became, overnight, a full-fledged purple martin mother.

"The third morning, unfortunately, the smaller of the two babies was found dead on the bottom of the cage. It is possible that he sustained a hidden injury from his fall from the house. That same day, a much smaller martin was found under the house, wet and shivering after a heavy rain and drop in temperature. We held him in our cupped hands until he was warm. He turned out to be a complete extrovert, accepting food eagerly and appearing to respond to soft conversation. Within a week, baby martin number one was sitting on the perch, legs and feet straight and strong, visibly looking for larger worlds to conquer, so we transferred both to a larger flight cage made of chicken wire top and sides with hardware cloth bottom. This cage is about four feet long, two feet wide, and two feet deep with a top which opens completely. We have put perches across, a few feet apart.

"Soon baby number one was flying happily from perch to perch. Baby number two thought, 'What fun!' and joined him, at least on the perch. Baby number one had now become a sociable little guy, deciding that 'if you can't lick 'em, join 'em.' He cocked his head when spoken to and stretched his bill toward our faces. He then would peck at our noses.

"Thinking to further his training, my husband fashioned a cross piece on top of a long bamboo pole, which he could place in a buried metal pipe in the ground just beside the martin house. When the baby was placed on this cross piece and raised high in the air, the excitement was tremendous. We did this in the evening when the elder martins were lined up on a nearby telephone wire, chatting about the state of the world.

"Immediately, they flew in ever-converging circles about the little fellow, who sat there in obvious ecstasy with his big new world. Some of the old martins flew within a foot of our baby, uttering what I can only think were warnings about his suspicious associations with humans. Finally, the baby made up his mind and took off, flying into a tree about 25 feet away. When retrieved and brought back to the cage, he expressed his fury by biting at us all the way.

"The following day, while feeding the younger baby a morsel, our venturesome adolescent suddenly took off straight up and off into the wild blue yonder. Later that evening, we saw him, all alone, in the top of a tall pine, preening his feathers. We watched through binoculars and were astonished to see him take off, flying high in large circles, soaring with the wind in glorious freedom. The next night we saw a baby martin, just his size and age, sitting alone on the roof of a neighbor's house near our martin house, looking wistfully at the elders gossiping on the wire. We hope that instinct took over and that he learned to feed himself.

"In the meanwhile, 'back at the ranch,' the second baby did a complete about-face. From a cheery, talkative little fellow, strong and healthy, he became morose, refusing to open his mouth for food and spitting out most of what was force-fed. Instead of sitting on his perch, he lay flat on the bottom of the cage, wings spread out, head down, and eyes closed.

"Just as we decided that death was imminent, a neighbor called me to rescue a baby cardinal that had evidently fallen from the nest prematurely and was abandoned by the parents. The cardinal was feathered but tiny, limp, and in a very bad condition. I placed him in the small cage with the martin, sure both would be dead in the morning. I managed to force bits of food in both before going to bed.

"Imagine, then, my joy in the morning to find both birds on the perch, huddled as close together as possible and both mouths open yelling for food! From then on, both birds maintained this closeness, the cardinal often perched on the back of the larger martin. Sometimes the cardinal opened his mouth and followed the martin as though adopting him as his mother.

"The martin flew about the cage, again a healthy bird. One day, the cage being open at feeding time, the martin suddenly flew out, with all the skill of a grown bird, soaring off in the sky. To our knowledge, we never saw him again.

"The cardinal, then called Chee-chee, appeared unhappy for a day. Then he, too, began flying about the cage. It became evident that if we did not want to climb to the top of the pines to feed him when the inevitable release date came, we would have to teach Chee-chee to come to us for food. He soon learned to pick up bits of food from our hands and sip water by himself. Several times, he came to us. We have allowed him the freedom of the screened porch for this purpose.

"This morning, we released him. All day, he has stayed in the trees in the yard, calling me when he is hungry, and coming to me to be fed. Since he will undoubtedly stay here all winter, he will be a most satisfactory pet.

As with all tame birds, there is always the great danger of accident, since he is fearless. He has become used to being sniffed by our small poodle, and I am in a quandary as to how to teach him the difference between an amiable poodle and a predatory cat."

Hazel Green, bird columnist of the Travis Audubon Society of Austin, Texas, told the story of "Cheepie," the little martin who thought she was "people:"

"Now Mr. Nolan Cloud, of Paradise Valley on the Blanco River in Wimberley, knows that young wild things should be left alone for their parents to manage. But last year, after a fledgling purple martin fell out of or was rejected from the nest three different times and he replaced it on the martin box each time, he decided that if the martins didn't want that baby, he did. So began the delightful episode of "Papa" Cloud and his foster "daughter," Cheepie.

"He soon realized that he had taken over no small job, and he became Papa Cloud to his neighbors. So for five weeks he and his cooperating neighbors caught insects, mostly grasshoppers, to appease the ravenous appetite of this tiny cheeping bird which Mr. Cloud named Cheepie. By the end of that time, she was beautifully covered with feathers, and since the normal nesting and feeding is from 24 to 28 days, he thought it was time she got out on her own. After much coaxing, Cheepie was persuaded to fly, and after awhile she learned to catch most of her own food. But she did love those handouts, especially early in the morning. If the Clouds were a little late on arising, around she'd fly until she found someone stirring who was willing to help her catch her breakfast.

"At first Cheepie made no effort to join up with the other martins. She simply felt like she was 'people.' She mingled freely with all the neighbors of Paradise Valley

209

and paid no attention to her own kind. In a gathering, she could always pick out Mr. Cloud and would perch on his shoulder and look up in his face and cheep. She loved to perch on his pipe and on the nozzle of the hose while he watered the garden. She wasn't taught any of her endearing tricks—they just seemed to come natural with her. She was the pride and joy of Paradise Valley last summer. Mr. Cloud has movies recording Cheepie's life with them.

"Toward the end of the summer, when Nature decreed that the time had come to begin their trip to Brazil for the winter, she made numerous attempts to join the martin colony before she was finally accepted. When the last of the colony left, Cheepie went along, and some of the charm went out of the lives of the folks in Paradise Valley. Will Cheepie return with the colony this year, and if so will she perch on the shoulder and pipe for her foster 'Papa' Cloud?"

Many others who have raised young martins have watched them depart in the fall with the same questions in mind. Although martins are known to return year after year to the same neighborhoods, it appears that in such cases they do not often return to their former status as pets.

One of the most notable experiences in the Griggsville area occurred in 1964, when the two children of Mr. and Mrs. C. I. Bethel of Pearl, in southeast Pike County, raised six stranded baby martins to maturity. The birds followed the Bethel children wherever they went and would pose for photographs on a stick held by the children. Kept in a box during the early weeks, the martins often would leave the box and enter the room where the children were watching television, where they sat on the rug watching the children.

The children had no metal bands, so they tied pieces

of string to the martins' legs before departure time in late summer. Whether the string was lost during the birds' travel or whether the birds did not return to Pearl, the children never knew, for their birds did not return to them the following spring.

But one notable case in which a befriended martin did return the following spring was reported from St. Louis, Missouri. Marie and Louis Schlueter spend their weekends at a cottage on a peninsula between the Mississippi and Illinois Rivers north of St. Louis, where they have a colony that averages 36 pairs.

They dearly love their martins, and Mrs. Schlueter has climbed trees, waded in muck, even been nipped by a snake rescuing young martins either in danger of falling into the water or already in it. She has successfully raised four sets, a total of 31 martins.

Of these, at least one remembered her kindness. This was a bird she raised in 1964 and marked with red nail polish under his tail. In the spring of 1965, the marked bird came home, and Mrs. Schlueter wrote, "I was so happy he came back and he flew low around me quite a few times. I was jumping around with joy. Anyone who would have seen me would probably have thought I was losing my marbles!"

In 1965, a purple martin was hit by a car in Griggsville and suffered a broken wing. The biology students of Griggsville High School took the injured martin under their collective wing and nursed it back to health. This martin, nicknamed "Handsome," recovered and rejoined the other martins in the Purple Martin Capital. It is one of the few cases on record in Griggsville in which other than young birds have been hand fed and returned to the flocks. One of the most remarkable stories on file is that of Mrs. Ramby Rasmussen of Newport, Minnesota, in the following chapter.

211

The stories of people and their martins are endless. This bird is a curious mixture of traits that enable it to develop a working friendship with man and yet maintain its instinctive devotion to age-old habits of migration and feeding.

CHAPTER XIII
THE CARE AND FEEDING OF MARTINS

In view of the widespread desire to increase the martin population in this country and in view of the martins' vulnerability to cold weather and of the young birds' being stranded on the ground, the art of hand-feeding has become a growing concern for martin fanciers.

Finding a suitable technique for rescuing adult birds and nursing them back to health is becoming equally important.

The care and feeding of young martins, while difficult, is not impossible. There are many successful case histories to prove this. Cases involving the successful feeding of older birds are less frequent but still occur.

Perhaps the most impressive experience in the feeding of older birds is that of Dr. and Mrs. Ramby Rasmussen of Newport, Minnesota. In 1950, the Rasmussens rescued 34 birds from their colony and nursed many of them back to health.

The martins arrived April 8 that year. It looked as though spring had come, with temperatures around the 50-degree mark. In a short time, however, the St. Paul Audubon Society reported martins suffering from starvation.

The Rasmussens lowered their house and carried the birds into their sun porch. Some were caught as they flew weakly around the yard.

Of the 34 brought indoors, eight were so weak they died overnight.

Mrs. Rasmussen fed the other refugees bits of hamburger and soft raisins. The martin house and the birdbath were moved to the sun porch. Light gauze curtains were draped over the windows to permit ample light without danger of the birds beating themselves against the glass. A half-dozen of the weakest birds were placed in an empty canary cage in the living room, where it was warmer.

It wasn't long until some of the birds were able to mount the perch in the cage, while the others cocked their heads in animated interest. By the time two or three good warm days brought out the flying insects, the martins were ready to release.

The great problem in saving adult martins from starvation is their exclusive diet of flying insects. Martins do not recognize as food any object that is not flying. Over the years, some species with similar diets—the tree swallow, for example—have learned to subsist on berries and other foods part of the time, but not the martin. It must have flying insects or die.

While this sometimes poses a great problem in finding ways to prevent the death by starvation of large numbers of the birds sometimes, it is by the same token one of man's greatest blessings. The fact that the martin cannot learn to subsist on non-insect food insures that it will remain effective as one of nature's most efficient air-cleaners and insect-controllers.

Raising young martins that have fallen from their nests is not only a way in which the birds' population can be substantially increased, but is a fascinating hobby as well. For the benefit of those who wish to join the thousands who already enjoy giving the birds a hand, we include here some foods that have been used in successful efforts to raise martins. Although a particular diet alone will not insure the survival of a young bird, the foods listed here will give martin enthusiasts a tested guide.

Calvin Break of Cape Girardeau, Missouri, used hamburger and occasionally a couple of drops of water. He served the hamburger on the rounded end of a toothpick and tried to duplicate the parents' meal schedule by feeding the young most heavily in the morning and evening.

Charles Butler of Arkansas City, Kansas, also recommends raw hamburger or dog food with a little water dispensed from an eyedropper.

Lovell Peterson of LaFayette, Illinois, used a toothpick to feed his martins a diet of lean ground round steak, hard boiled eggs, fish worms, and grasshoppers.

As noted earlier in this book, Mrs. John Vosburg of Salamanca, New York, used an exclusive diet of grasshoppers.

The J. D. Turnbaughs of Grandview, Missouri, used the yolks of boiled eggs plus packaged dried insects.

The biology class of Griggsville High School used a variety of insects and spiders but relied principally on hamburger.

Frank L. Mills of Canfield, Ohio, successfully used egg yolks, liver, and an occasional bug.

Mrs. Roy Nedderman of Sunman, Indiana, used hamburger, cottage cheese, soft raisins, and water, and employed her electric bug catcher to snare the real thing for them.

Mrs. Lawrence Zeleny, whose experiences are recounted elsewhere in this book, used a mixture of ground steak, di-calcium phosphate containing vitamin D, a small puppy biscuit shaved fine, and Pervinal, a vitamin-mineral mixture designed for puppies. She also used boiled egg yolk, cooked liver, and water.

Regina Lapitz of La Crosse, Wisconsin, added sugar water to the list of foods used successfully in raising young martins.

To help the birds remain active, Harold Hassman of Appleton, Wisconsin, put a light bulb in his bird house. Unfortunately, there is no artificial way to keep the martins' natural food supply equally active during cold weather.

215

Dr. William J. Beecher, director of the Chicago Academy of Sciences, noted the severe loss of martins in the Chicago area caused by the erratic spring weather of 1966 and said the loss would be a disadvantage of Chicagoans because of the birds' mosquito-eating capacity.

Dr. Beecher outlined emergency action to help the birds. He suggested that rescuers keep the birds indoors and warm for a few days and force-feed them, adding that the birds will be too weak to object.

The procedure he suggested is to take the bird in your left hand and, holding its back against your chest, use your left thumbnail to press the lower bill and pull it down. Then poke a pea-sized pellet of food down the bird's throat with your right index finger. "If you just drop it in his mouth he'll choke," Dr. Beecher cautioned.

He emphasized that martins must be released after they are strong enough to fly and fend for themselves. It is, in fact, against the law to keep one except in an emergency. Martins not only prefer freedom—they can do more good patrolling our neighborhoods for insects than they can as indoor pets.

CHAPTER XIV
THE CITY MARTIN: HIS DAY IN THE COURTS

We have often heard bird fanciers "waxing poetic," but never a district judge who then, in a court of law, "found" against the purple martins!

It happened in Des Moines, Iowa, in the autumn of 1964. As related by a number of newspapers in the area, a gentleman who liked purple martins and who had managed to attract a colony of 150-200 birds to his martin houses was hailed into court by another gentleman who worked the night shift in a meat-packing plant and who was kept awake by the daytime chatter of the busy martins. It seems that the plaintiff's lack of sleep made him irritable and caused marital discord.

The judge, in limiting the defendant to no more than two martin houses containing no more than 20 apartments, poetized from the bench as follows:

"Martin, martin, purple martin, art thou, when in numbers assembled, a nuisance?

"Several witnesses have praised thy song. Thy activities are described as beneficial, that thou feedest upon insects and thereby thou destroyest many hated mosquitoes and pests.

"Thou art a natural insecticide and pesticide much safer than man's chemical wares, and thereby mishaps and other dangers as pointed out in *Silent Spring* are avoided. Thy industry and clean habits have won the approval of our federal government . . . so that thou hast become one of its protected migratory birds.

"Conservationists praise thy work and favor the destruction of less desirable species of birds.

"Many of thy friends have erected houses with numerous

apartments for thy occupancy. Thy presence gladdens their hearts and acts as a therapeutic to some of them, reduces their tensions and causes relaxation.

"But thy objectors maintain that when thou and many more like thee assemble, thy vocalizations are far from being pleasant music, prevent workers weary with toil from going to sleep, and such irritation has caused domestic friction.

"Thy droppings soil their clothes when out on the clothesline, soil their cars, their outdoor furniture and deprive them of uninterrupted sunbathing and prevent barbecuing in their back yard as formerly was their wont."

From the last remarks of our tongue-in-cheek judge, we would assume that neither he nor any of the witnesses testifying for the plaintiff in this particular case know the difference between the martin and the starling.

For the martin enthusiasts of the nation, there still is a story to be told and a job to be done.

5-YEAR RECORD ON MARTIN HABITS

First Year: 19_____

Date martin house installed_____

Type of house_____

Number of compartments_____

Height above ground_____

Distance from nearest building_____

Distance from nearest trees_____

House installed where?   City_____ Suburban_____ Rural_____

Distance to nearest body of water_____

Arrival date of martin scouts_____

Arrival date of main flock_____

Number of martins occupying house_____

Number of sparrows occupying house_____

Date young martins hatched_____

Date flock left_____

Noticeable relief from insects after martins arrive? _____

Other martin houses in the immediate area? _____

Other data of interest: _____

_____

_____

_____

_____

_____

5-YEAR RECORD ON MARTIN HABITS

Second Year: 19_____

Date martin house installed_____

Type of house_____

Number of compartments_____

Height above ground_____

Distance from nearest building_____

Distance from nearest trees_____

House installed where?   City_____ Suburban_____ Rural_____

Distance to nearest body of water_____

Arrival date of martin scouts_____

Arrival date of main flock_____

Number of martins occupying house_____

Number of sparrows occupying house_____

Date young martins hatched_____

Date flock left_____

Noticeable relief from insects after martins arrive? _____

Other martin houses in the immediate area? _____

Other data of interest: _____

_____

_____

_____

_____

_____

5-YEAR RECORD ON MARTIN HABITS

Third Year: 19_____

Date martin house installed_____

Type of house_____

Number of compartments_____

Height above ground_____

Distance from nearest building_____

Distance from nearest trees_____

House installed where?   City_____ Suburban_____ Rural_____

Distance to nearest body of water_____

Arrival date of martin scouts_____

Arrival date of main flock_____

Number of martins occupying house_____

Number of sparrows occupying house_____

Date young martins hatched_____

Date flock left_____

Noticeable relief from insects after martins arrive? _____

Other martin houses in the immediate area? _____

Other data of interest: _____

_____

_____

_____

_____

_____

5-YEAR RECORD ON MARTIN HABITS

Fourth Year: 19_____

Date martin house installed_____

Type of house_____

Number of compartments_____

Height above ground_____

Distance from nearest building_____

Distance from nearest trees_____

House installed where?   City_____ Suburban_____ Rural_____

Distance to nearest body of water_____

Arrival date of martin scouts_____

Arrival date of main flock_____

Number of martins occupying house_____

Number of sparrows occupying house_____

Date young martins hatched_____

Date flock left_____

Noticeable relief from insects after martins arrive? _____

Other martin houses in the immediate area? _____

Other data of interest: _____

_____

_____

_____

_____

_____

5-YEAR RECORD ON MARTIN HABITS

Fifth Year: 19_____

Date martin house installed_____

Type of house_____

Number of compartments_____

Height above ground_____

Distance from nearest building_____

Distance from nearest trees_____

House installed where?   City_____Suburban_____Rural_____

Distance to nearest body of water_____

Arrival date of martin scouts_____

Arrival date of main flock_____

Number of martins occupying house_____

Number of sparrows occupying house_____

Date young martins hatched_____

Date flock left_____

Noticeable relief from insects after martins arrive? _____

Other martin houses in the immediate area? _____

Other data of interest: _____

_____

_____

_____

_____

_____